This is a book for the real world. If you are hungry to change your organization, then read it and act on it.

*Seth Kybird, CEO, Nuclear Transport Solutions*

*Business Morphology* is a clever, succinct, aide memoire which neatly captures and brings to life five principal levers aimed at helping those looking to drive meaningful change within their organization. Whether you're a small business owner or the CEO of a large corporation, this book will help you navigate the complex world of business change, offering practical advice and real-world examples to help you succeed.

*Godfrey McFall, Chair, Oryxalign*

This is an engaging and practical guide which will be a welcome addition to the change management literature. Unlike some other texts, it avoids case studies based on mega enterprises or distant corporations which are irrelevant to most practitioners. In place, this is a readable and practical book that you can actually use!

*Alun Griffiths, Non-Executive Director*

Change is an unchanging fact of life, especially in business. No matter how carefully one tracks the growth of a commercial enterprise, change will happen, planned or otherwise. Navigating this is one of the real keys to business success. Here, Julie Nerney and Geoff Robins have used their decades of experience transforming businesses, or advising them in times of crisis, to provide the reader with invaluable commercial insight.

*Simon Elliott, Managing Director, Sentinel*

Successful change demands real clarity – and *Business Morphology* offers leaders just that. Leading change is knowing how to navigate through, and this totally readable book gives a path and plenty of ideas to follow. Successful change is down to people and their ability to engage, so it's great to see a chapter on maximizing personal impact. This excellent book is brimming with shared experiences, tips and how-to's for change leaders. 'Be purposeful, do interesting work, make a difference' – I couldn't agree more!

*Nick Diprose, Founding Partner, Holdsway*

If there's one thing that we can be certain about the coming years, there will be more change, and it will happen quicker than ever. Standing still is not an option, so businesses must learn to embrace this change. *Business Morphology* should be considered a key tool for business leaders to support that shift.

*Neil Witten, Adviser, Entrepreneur, Podcast Host and Author*

Delivering meaningful change is a daunting task, but this book provides a clear and concise roadmap for achieving it. The five-point framework and Morphology Maps presented in the book are rooted in solid, proven, best practice; but what sets this book apart is the authors' ability to translate theory into a highly practical and accessible guide based on their decades of real-world experience. The case studies are relevant and thought-provoking, and remind us again and again that change is about people... and planning! If you're looking for a roadmap to deliver meaningful change that actually works, this book is a great start point.

*David Ashcroft, Founder and Director, Stratex Plus*

*Business Morphology* offers the toolkit every business leader needs to navigate the complexities of change for their business in this rapidly changing world. It offers tangible solutions for approaching the many challenges that come with change. A must read.

*Lauren Grimwood, Global Director of Transformation, Kin+Carta*

*Business Morphology* is a great read for any business leader. It outlines what you must consider to effectively change your organization, but more importantly shares how to act on it to achieve the change. It lays out useful tools (I am already adopting Morphology Maps), outlines the key levers for change, and provides real world guidance in a way which is clear and digestible. It also puts a focus on culture which underpins all successful transformation activity. I look forward to applying much of this personally.

*Dan Wright, Founder and Managing Director, Monochrome Consultancy*

We are operating in a challenging environment, heavily reliant upon fast moving technology. However, the human factor has never been more important or indeed relevant as it is today. Organizations must constantly assess and then respond to those challenges. It is, in many instances, a metamorphosis of their business. This is why this highly intelligent and insightful book has an important message to impart to organizations who are committed to success through these challenging times.

*Allan Cook CBE DSc FREng,*
*Chairman, High Value Manufacturing Catapult*

Successful and effective change is difficult. This book distils the essence of the pillars of change (the 5 levers) and gives a smart tool through the Morphology Map to continually focus on the critical activities of the 'what' and 'who' of communication and engagement to really maximize success.

*Mike Luntz, Director Strategy and Transformation, World Rugby*

Whichever wise and learned person said change is a constant did not live in the 21st century. There is nothing constant about our pace of change. Every few years it is exponentially accelerated. For businesses, trying to keep up with the pace of change is no mean feat and you need tried and tested principles and frameworks that cut through and help you deliver value and progress. There is a wealth of information out there, but this book provides the signal through the noise and enables you to accelerate your own progress to deliver impactful change. A vital guide for transformation success.

*Lindsay Ratcliffe, Chief Product Officer – Europe, Kin+Carta*

# BUSINESS MORPHOLOGY

## HOW TO NAVIGATE THROUGH CHANGE

# JULIE NERNEY
# & GEOFF ROBINS

First published in Great Britain by Practical Inspiration Publishing, 2023

ISBN   9781788604741 (print)
       9781788604765 (epub)
       9781788604758 (mobi)

Want to bulk-buy copies of this book for your team and colleagues? We can customize the content and co-brand *Business Morphology* to suit your business's needs.

Please email info@practicalinspiration.com for more details.

Practical Inspiration
Publishing

# Contents

# Foreword

There's a huge volume of literature about change out there, including books, podcasts and articles in popular as well as serious academic journals. And, like me, you may be forgiven for thinking that much of it is either rather derivative or just not very helpful, so you might be wondering what another can add that is both useful and easy to put into practice. Well, here's a book that passes the test and is worth reading.

As Julie Nerney and Geoff Robins note, there are plenty of examples of organizations that, having failed to change, crashed and burned pretty spectacularly. There are also, no doubt, many more that are declining less dramatically but just as surely, as they fail to come to terms with change triggered by the familiar mix of technology, market shifts, political or regulatory decisions, as well as the less predictable jolts. So, it's not controversial to say that change is an important matter for all of us. Pretty much anyone who works in an organization, regardless of sector, size or geography, will have to deal more than once with the sometimes painful process of change as well as the consequences, and perhaps try to lead some sort of change during their working life.

For those who are leading change, the authors distil their own wide experience to identify what they see as five main levers to effect change and work through how to handle each of these. They avoid going over the usual distinctions between radical and incremental change (and the overworked transformation word) and instead they use the concept of morphology – which is concerned with the form or state of a phenomenon such as a business or other type of organization. So, change is about morphing – shifting from one form to another and the central theme of the book is how to morph successfully. Perhaps the most intriguing of these levers are people and culture, because they are usually the central objects of change as well as being levers of change. But understanding how to pull any of these (often interconnected) levers is complex and very important.

The book helps the reader by grounding this challenge in a deceptively simple way. The central idea, or proposition, is to have a plan. You might think this is self-evident – who would knowingly walk into a change episode without one? But planning effectively is never simple: plans need to be feasible, reasonably comprehensive and well-tested, while at the same time built on the assumption that as things will change as the process unfolds, they need to have flexibility built into them. I'm sure I am not alone in having seen plans that don't meet those criteria and therefore don't underpin change effectively.

I see this book as helping both with the feasibility and flexibility issues in the way that it helps planning to take place. It does so by focusing on what the authors call their Morphology Maps, a neat idea that encapsulates the discipline of thinking through what you can control and what you can't control, but can influence, to organize the composition of a plan. In other words, the book doesn't frame a plan as a detailed map of the process of change or make the mistake of trying to reduce the complex and dynamic reality of change into a simple linear process (which is where many other models fail). Rather, it helps you think about how you are going to address the various elements which will be embedded in that process, be they under your control or factors that you have to try and influence. And that is what makes this way of thinking about planning valuable. Sorting what might be called the wheat from the chaff in deciding what you control or have to influence allows you to plan effectively.

Framing the challenge as influencing (rather than things being beyond your control) is not only realistic, but also a very helpful contribution of this book. It reminds anyone leading change that you'll need an influence strategy. And to make that work, you'll need influencing skills focusing on what elements you need to try and influence, who will need to be influenced and who can help you influence others (in other words, your important allies). Of course, influencing may not always work or be entirely successful but it's important to map it and have a plan. Influence takes change leadership into the difficult and often politically fraught job of selling their vision, the rationale and thinking through how they can go some way to meeting the agendas of others. It requires skill, time and compromise but no change programme will succeed without what one might call influence-work. And, of course, when influencing is effective it basically expands the domain of control as well as generating confidence.

This is a valuable book for the way it frames change realistically. The Morphology Maps organize the chapters helpfully and it has advice and how-to suggestions as well as useful case studies and nuggets of wisdom that will engender confidence in any reader who has to lead change now or will in the future. Appropriately enough, the authors finish with a chapter on you – the reader – and how you can use the idea of a Morphology Map to think about your own future career. In that way, they nicely emphasize the sense of individual agency that runs throughout the book even when you have to deal with the most difficult challenges of change.

Tim Morris
*Emeritus Professor, Oxford Saïd Business School, 2023*

# Preface

## Why Morphology?

We thought long and hard about this, and realize that our use of the term *Morphology* may warrant an apology to the purists out there, but bear with us. The Collins English Dictionary definition of Morphology (n) is:

1. The branch of biology concerned with the form and structure in organisms.

2. The form and structure of words in a language, especially the consistent patterns of inflection, combination, derivation and change, that may be observed and classified.

3. The form and structure of anything.

When you consider that definition, this book is clearly not aimed at the biological or linguist aspects, but it is concerned with the form and structure of organizations and how their people, processes and systems interact together.

In particular, what propelled us to write this book was the desire to help leaders and managers navigate their way through changes to their organizations in a way that is as smooth as possible and delivers maximum impact and outcomes.

So, our use of the word Morphology, is a blend of two terms as cited in the Cambridge English Dictionary:

Morph (v): to gradually, change, or change someone or something, from one thing or another; and

Ology (n): Informal. A science or other branch of knowledge.

The combination of these is the foundation of this book, which seeks to address the core question facing leaders and managers everywhere: How do you change the form and structure of your organization for the better, and what are the important things you need to consider and plan for when doing it?

We are, of course, not claiming that this book is a scientific publication. But it is a source of knowledge based on over 75 years collective experience of changing organizations from one state to another. Sharing things we wish we'd known when we first encountered them. And some of the iterative learning that occurs from having done them multiple times, in different contexts and sectors. We want to save you getting the same battle scars as us, so you reach the outcomes that you want faster.

So, with apologies to the Biologists and the Linguists for high-jacking your definition – welcome to *Business Morphology*.

# Chapter 1
# Morphology Maps:
# Navigating change

*Standing still is the fastest way of moving backwards in a rapidly changing world.*

Lauren Bacall

## Introduction

Over the past ten years the list of major organizations that have gone out of business is staggering. They cover all sectors of the industrial landscape, and include household names such as Kodak, Toys R Us, Blockbuster, Tower Records, Woolworths, the list goes on. Even where elements of these brands have survived, they do so under a very different business model. And although Lauren Bacall was best known as a great American film star, her words of wisdom remain true today as they ever were.

Of course, the reason for the failure of each of these organizations is complicated and driven by a range of events including rapid market shifts, new technology advancements and global financial issues. However, the common thread when you read any of the reflections on what went wrong for these organizations, is that they were slow to fully recognize the threats in front of them, and slow to react. The truth of the matter is that in today's global and interconnected marketplace, if you are to survive and thrive – irrespective of your starting point – standing still is not an option. Your business must continue to evolve and adapt over time to stay relevant and competitive.

# Context for this book

We know from our extensive experience of designing and leading change, that altering the way in which an organization operates, is structured or works, can be described in a range of different ways. It could be branded a change programme, or badged with the increasingly over used label of transformation. In our opinion what these terms express are two ends of a spectrum: a transformation is something that can never revert to its former state – like a caterpillar turning into a butterfly – whereas a change is something that could be reversed or replaced, like a system or process update.

Irrespective of where you sit on this spectrum, in the context of this book we describe any implementation of change as morphing – changing from one state to another as seamlessly as possible, at a pace that is dictated by the environment in which you find yourself.

This is not a one-off activity. Organizations are constantly adapting and evolving, and you should consider each time you morph as a wave of change that creates a new foundation for the next one – like the way a volcano shapes its landscape. An eruption creates a high impact change as the molten lava flows, but this lava then solidifies and creates a new state, until the next eruption. A volcano is never done, and as a result the surrounding area morphs over time. This is the same principle for organizational change – albeit it on a much shorter timescale. Morph, let those changes settle, look over your shoulder at how far you've come, celebrate that achievement, then morph again.

The reasons for the need to morph from one state to another are varied. Disruptions in the market or context in which your business operates may necessitate hard defensive choices to ensure survival. Alternatively, unexpected openings may appear as a result of emerging technology, which create both the opportunity and environment for your business to succeed. Whatever the reason, if change is required, a plan of action is needed, and this book is designed to help you do just that – plan and successfully navigate your way through change.

# Business Morphology Maps

The process of change can be complex, challenging and even daunting. Business Morphology is here to help break down this complexity so that you can start to put together a coherent and realistic plan of what to do and when. At the heart of *Business Morphology* are the Morphology Maps, which are an easy to use, visual tool to help guide your thinking and prioritization.

The start point for the creation of a Map is the desired outcomes you are seeking to achieve. This will be triggered by a range of considerations but will be based upon the key metrics that you use to manage and run your business. For example, falling profit while maintaining revenue could suggest that your organization is becoming less efficient; falling sales could indicate that you need to consider what you are selling and how you are doing it compared with your competitors; an increase in staff turnover and decrease in staff engagement might require you to consider your approach to how you are attracting and retaining your people. Any of these examples should result in making changes that reverse these trends. However, your desired outcomes could equally be driven by a proactive strategy that is geared to increasing shareholder value. Typically, this will result in a desire to accelerate growth by moving into different markets or by undertaking a merger or acquisition.

So, identifying what you want to achieve is at the heart of selecting the change lever (or levers) you need to employ to achieve the outcomes you require; and irrespective of what levers you pull, you need a plan of action that will get you there. To assist in building that plan of action the Morphology Maps are constructed around two simple axes: things that you can control and things that you must seek to influence.

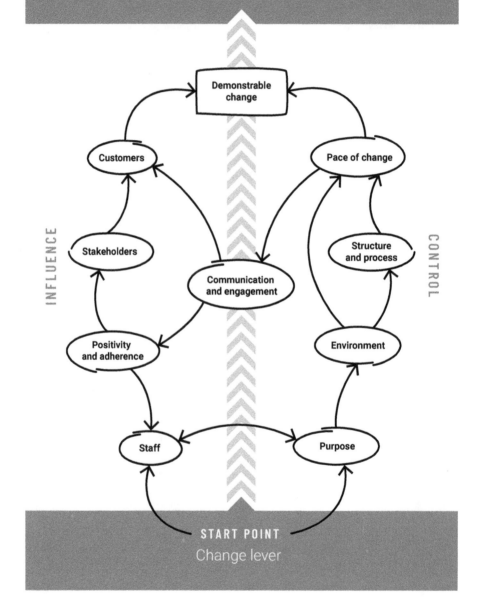

Of these two axes, defining the things you can control is clearly the easiest to do and, irrespective of the change lever you select there will be some fundamental components that will always be part of this side of the Map:

- Ensuring that you understand the core purpose of your organization and the outcomes you are seeking to achieve from any changes you embark on.

- Activities that enable you to understand the environment you are operating in and the factors you need to take into consideration when changing.

- The need to ensure your structure and organization is correctly aligned to your purpose and direction.

- Changes that are designed to optimize the efficiency of your processes, systems and people.

But these activities cannot be pursued in isolation. All organizations have their own internal ecosystems and they operate within a large and complex external environment. Much of this is difficult to understand, and even more difficult to control. This is where the influence side of the Morphology Map comes to the fore. In any change activity there are a range of stakeholders that need to be communicated with, engaged and influenced. This can range from your own staff, through to customers and stakeholders that you might not have met yet. Understanding who the key stakeholders are is a critical element of the influence side of any Morphology Map.

To bring this to life each of the key activities on the control side of the Map, or the key stakeholder groups on the influence side of the Map, are drawn as a separate elements with an appropriate description. Each element is then joined to others via a series of arrows in order to show the potential inter-relationship that will exist between them. In some cases this will be because some elements will be dependent on others taking place first. In other cases the inter-relationship will be enduring but its importance may vary over time.

And it is your communication and engagement activities that join the two sides of the Map together. They are not only the pivot for each of the Maps presented in this book but they are also essential to the success of the changes you are seeking to make. These communication and engagement activities need to be as comprehensive as possible, recognizing that there will be timing and complexity considerations for each of the different audiences. And, like every part of your plan, you will want to iterate and modify these activities over time based on the feedback you receive.

## Foundation for your plan of action

It is important to note that a Morphology Map is not your plan. The power of the Map is to help you identify the things that are important to consider so that they form the foundation of a rigorous plan of who does what, and when, to get to your desired outcomes.

The Map is at the heart of guiding you to prioritize your time and energy on the right things with the right level of detail to address specific areas of concern or risk. Every plan will be entirely dependent on the scenario your organization finds itself in.

And, of course, as the saying goes, no plan survives contact with the enemy. Your plan should be dynamic and iterative. As you progress through the actions you've determined you need, take a moment to pause to think about what impact it has had. This reflection will help you continually refocus to get the outcomes you want in the most effective way.

## Change levers

Having determined the need to change and the outcomes you want to achieve, the start point for any Morphology Map is the identification of the most appropriate change lever. In our experience, there are five fundamental levers that can be applied to effect real change in an organization. We can say this with confidence because when we look back over the dozens of change initiatives we've both been involved in, they all come back to one or more of these five levers. They are:

1. Modifying your operating model
2. Product or service diversification
3. Mergers or acquisitions
4. People
5. Culture

So, which of these levers do you need to apply to ensure you achieve the outcome you require? Most people will naturally focus on the first three levers of modifying their operating model, product or service diversification, or more radically, merger or acquisition.

They will also naturally tend towards wanting to minimize risk, which lends itself to starting with modifying your operating model because it is internally focused and so is perceived as being easier to control. Whereas product or service diversification, or pursuing a merger or acquisition could be transformational, and will inevitably involve a range of external factors. Modifying your operating model could increase your efficiency and improve your margin, but the second two could do that as well as increasing top line revenue and market share.

Whatever your choice, the risk scale increases as you move through these three options and, in the process, you start to differentiate between change and transformation. Whichever part of the risk spectrum you are on, and whichever of these three levers you chose to employ, it is important to note that they rarely operate in isolation. For example, implementing product or service diversification, or pursuing a merger or acquisition, will probably necessitate modifications to your operating model. And irrespective of the lever selected, there will always be an impact on the people in the organization and its underlying culture.

It would be understandable to view the first three of the five change levers as tangible and the latter two of people and culture as intangible. But experience has taught us that people and culture are powerful levers in their own right, as well as important elements of driving the outcomes you want from the other levers. You can have the most efficient operating model and product or service range, but without the right people, with the right skills, experience and attitude to deliver those outcomes, the business will fail. People are at the heart of any business and creating an environment that enables them to do the right thing, at the right time, is fundamental to success.

Likewise for culture – too often described as a soft subject and given to the HR team to manage. Your culture is the single biggest accelerant for the performance of your business that you can deploy. And indeed, the single biggest brake on progress if you get it wrong. If two organizations have the same infrastructure and resources at their disposal, the culture within their organization is the differentiator. *What* you do matters, but *how* you do it creates a performance advantage.

As the illustration below shows, whichever primary lever you choose to use, it will inevitably result in needing to consider activities associated with some or all of the other levers as you build your plan.

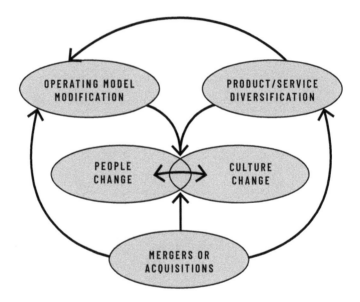

## Structure and sectors

Our motivation in writing this book is to help you navigate your way through change in a way that is as smooth as possible, delivering maximum impact and your desired outcomes. To that end, each of the five change levers are considered in the following chapters of the book.

For each one we have developed a Morphology Map which identifies the things you should consider as you construct your plan, based on our collective experience of what does and doesn't work. Each Map is accompanied by a narrative which brings it to life in terms of why the control and influence elements included in the Maps, and their various inter-relationships, matter. This narrative is supported by case studies with insights into where each change lever has, or has not, been successful, providing valuable learning as you prepare your plan.

Each of the five change levers is a topic in its own right, and there are a wealth of books and other materials available on all of them. The Morphology Maps and associated text are not exhaustive, nor have they been designed to be so. Rather, they reflect the critical factors we think are important when implementing your plans for each of the levers.

By and large the content of this book is written through the lens of private sector organizations, but the concept of Morphology and the five levers of change identified are truly sector agnostic. They can (and have been) applied in the public, private and third sectors. Of course, the context will be different, but the fundamentals remain the same. Every organization needs to run in the most efficient way possible, providing products or services which meet the needs of their customers. Structural change can take place in any sector, with the public and third sectors increasingly using mergers to drive cost savings or greater societal impact. And of course, people and culture matter to every organization if it is to achieve its outcomes.

# Leadership

As you read the book, it is important to keep front of mind that whatever lever you pull, successful change takes leadership. Morphing from one state to another is challenging, and the best performing organizations are those with exceptional leaders who have the right experience at the right time for that point in the life cycle of the business. Good leaders listen and involve others in defining the direction for their organization. They have first class communication skills. They provide clarity, promote confidence, build empathy and trust. And they address both the control and influence sides of the Morphology Map with equal focus. This enables them to create followership, taking their people with them and building teams who work cohesively together. Ensuring you have the right leadership for the change you are embarking on is critical to the success of your plan.

## An added bonus

In addition to the change lever chapters, we have also included a chapter focused on you, the individual. Because ultimately, wherever you are in an organization, you're either leading or taking part in change. This Map and associated narrative will enable you to reflect on how you maximize your contribution to your organization, and your chances of achieving the aspirations you have for your own career. The same principles apply – there will be things you can control and things you must seek to influence. And you still need a plan – you might revisit it and update it, but having a plan is the constant across all of the Maps.

And for those of you itching to get on with building a plan to drive the changes your organization needs, our Epilogue provides you with some practical principles on how to go about this too – all designed to help you reach the outcomes you aspire to.

Happy planning!

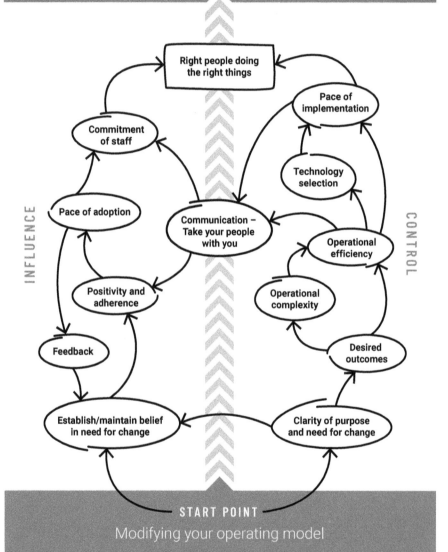

**DESIRED OUTCOMES**
- Increased efficiency
- Improved clarity
- Optimised size/shape
- Increased profit

Right people doing
the right things

Pace of
implementation

Commitment
of staff

Technology
selection

INFLUENCE

CONTROL

Pace of adoption

Communication –
Take your people
with you

Operational
efficiency

Positivity and
adherence

Operational
complexity

Feedback

Desired
outcomes

Establish/maintain belief
in need for change

Clarity of purpose
and need for change

**START POINT**
Modifying your operating model

# Chapter 2
# Modifying your operating model

*If you don't drive your business, you will be driven out of business.*

B. C. Forber

## Introduction

At its simplest, an operating model is a description of the people, processes and systems that make your business tick. Understanding these core components and how they interact is vital to ensuring your business is operating efficiently.

The old adage 'if it isn't broken don't fix it' is undoubtedly true. But as B. C. Forber implies, complacency is simply not an option. There is an almost continuous pressure for every organization to operate more efficiently, and to maintain or improve profit margins. Increasing efficiency requires absolute clarity on what and how you are spending your time, effort and money on now (the as-is state) and then identifying where changes are required to save time, effort and money in the future (the to-be state or target operating model).

So what are the things you need to consider when you are modifying your operating model?

## Clarify your purpose

At the macro level every organization has a mission, but more importantly exists for a specific purpose. Understanding and clarifying that purpose is at the heart of how you design your operating model –

the *how* must follow on from the *why* and the *what*. If you've made the decision that you need to change the way your organization operates, it is vital that you pursue this in the context of a deep understanding of your core purpose.

There are many examples of multinational businesses with very sophisticated purpose statements. But when we talk about purpose, that's not what we're not referring to. For us, it's about ensuring that you understand *why* you are doing what you do. It requires you to really understand who your customers are. What do they want? What's important to them that makes them use you? And how are you going to deliver the goods and services they need?

The answers to these questions should drive the design of your operating model. For example, if your customers are coming to you motivated by price and speed of delivery, it tells you that your cost of production should be minimized and your delivery process optimized – your organization has to be lean and mean. However, if your customers are motivated by quality, and price is not a defining factor, it tells you that you should spend time, energy and money on your brand and educating potential customers on why your goods or services are of a higher quality when compared to your competitors.

This understanding of what is important to you – and more importantly your customers – should be treated as your *North Star*. If you are to successfully modify your operating model in any way, it must be in service of this. Every decision you make should be taken in light of the outcome you are aiming for. Without this discipline, you run the risk of making excellent isolated decisions, but when you look at them through the lens of your North Star, you may find yourself wishing you'd made slightly different choices to better align to that gravitational pull. Clarity on purpose and outcomes is the starting point for your plan, and it makes individual decision points much easier to navigate along the way.

# Case study: Failing to find your North Star

A medium-sized private sector organization sought external support to help the senior team understand why their change programme hadn't delivered the desired results.

Less than a year previously, the senior leadership team had recognized that there were efficiency savings to be made in how the organization was operating, which could both improve their profit margin and employee experience. As a result, the organization had been through a process of re-defining its values with its employees, one of which had been about a seamless internal and external customer experience, and it was clear from feedback that wasn't the reality for people. The senior team had received countless pieces of feedback about how painful it was to get even the simplest things done. Everything from raising a purchase order through to basic self-service HR administration.

The approach of the senior leadership team had been to encourage high levels of ownership of the changes required to tackle this, and each functional area in the business had been asked to nominate a leader for the work. This person was largely released from their day job to create the capacity to look at how the processes and systems in their area were working now (the as-is), where the opportunities for improvement were (the to-be) and then work with their teams to implement them. If improvements required investment, they could make a case to the senior team for funding.

On the face of it this looks to have all the hallmarks of the things you should consider when embarking on any changes – the requirements were clearly identified, the resources put in place rather than expecting people to do things in the margins of their day job, the end users were empowered to be part of the changes, and there was a route to securing any investment, if it was required.

The 20 individual leads had cracked on with their plans which rolled out at different rates depending on the complexity of the change. To give a flavour of the range of timescales for the different components, updated policies and procedures appeared on the intranet in just a few weeks for people to access; whereas it took nine months to implement a new finance system.

In less than a year every functional lead was claiming success, but the same anecdotal feedback was still coming through to the senior team. Things still weren't working optimally. That's when they asked for external support to help them understand why they hadn't got the outcomes they were expecting. And it was all down to the lack of any North Star.

They had done what so many organizations do, which is to pursue operating model changes in functional isolation. The nominated leads had all ploughed excellent furrows, but in complete disregard of what others were doing. Even where processes spanned different functional areas, such as the purchase-to-pay process (which started with budget holding teams, then went to procurement, and then finance) the changes had been pursued around only the elements in one function.

The simple fact was the root cause for the programme failure was because the senior leadership had initiated the changes at a level of operational detail before having first shaped the strategic and enabling components which should precede this.

Rectifying this required the organization to first of all reaffirm its purpose, which then fed their strategy, brand and culture. Collectively, this then became their North Star for the second try in redesigning their operating model. Every decision in each functional area now had to align around their core purpose. They quickly saw the cost of having pursued the changes in isolation: choices that looked sensible as a stand-alone decision now demanded a different answer in the context of the North Star.

This alignment underpinned their new change programme which saw them revisit over 90 percent of the scope that they had delivered in the past year – everything from end-to-end processes across the organization, through to the need to reverse previous system implementations which had seemed liked a good idea at the time. This all amounted to a significant sunk cost and delay in delivering the margin improvement they had hoped for two years previously.

Operating model changes will fail if you don't have clarity on your purpose and outcomes – if you can't articulate your North Star don't start until you can.

# The need for change

Defining your North Star doesn't just provide clarity on the outcomes you need and a framing point for individual decisions, it also enables you to easily articulate the need for change to your people. In the case study above, it was the employees themselves who had identified the need for change. But this isn't always the case, and making sure that your people can see why the change is needed can be very challenging.

People's response to change is largely emotional, and so it is important that when you make the case for change you use objective data points and facts to take the emotion out of the decision. This could be falling sales, a drop in profit margin, an increase in the costs of doing business due to external factors, or the arrival of a new competitor. But even doing that won't be sufficient to counter the emotional response. It needs good quality storytelling or a narrative arc to connect with that emotion, which is the start point for the influencing side of the Morphology Map.

Let's bring this to life. It is not uncommon for business leaders who live and breathe their data to only focus on the logic of the situation they are facing. The result: a management pronouncement that says profits have been falling for six months. So there is a need to focus on cost reduction and they want every team to look for better, faster ways of doing things as a matter of urgency. Inevitably this message is translated into job cuts in the minds of the staff, breeding fear and uncertainty.

Now imagine the situation being handled in a way which ensures the person delivering the message puts themselves in the shoes of their audience and seeks to influence rather than tell.

That might look like a more engaging story about the journey that the business has been on, its many successes along the way, the changing context that they are now operating in, some data points about how that is playing out in business performance, before going on to articulate the direction required for the next phase of the business to counter these headwinds. And how everyone can play their part, an opportunity to not only be part of an exciting change programme but gain new skills and experience in the process.

Sure, that's an overly simplistic comparison to make the point, but it's where you and your leadership team need to start if you are to make any modification to your operating model. It would be easy to see this as a mechanistic process and system driven change: a simple internal lever to pull where you can focus on the control side of the Map and get immediate results.

But without sufficient attention to that first step on the influence side of the Map where you begin to establish and then maintain the belief in the need for change, then there will be a drag factor on every other element on the influence side. Change adoption will be low, morale will suffer and the compliance and commitment to the new ways of working from your people won't be there. The simple fact is the leadership team needs to influence, both at the outset and throughout the change programme, if it is to deliver the required outcomes.

## Define your outcomes

Any successful change programme keeps four things in focus throughout – design, delivery, change and benefits. By that, we mean being clear about the root cause of the problem and the requirements to fix that before rushing in, making sure you have the right capacity and capability to make it happen, making sure that you bring people on the change journey from the outset, and being clear about the benefits of why you are doing something.

In our experience, these are often treated as linear steps rather than a dynamic or iterative process over the change journey. And none more so than benefits. Traditionally this has been a tool which is used to make the case for investment up front. The principal driver of why it's worth it – because by spending *x*, we'll save or generate *y*. The numbers are always based on assumptions and the only certain thing about them is that they will be wrong – unless you have a crystal ball and can see the future. But in the absence of that, it is an educated guess at a set point in time. And because things change and the numbers lose their credibility there is a tendency to stop focusing on benefits.

But this is a narrow view of benefits. There will be financial benefits – especially with operating model changes which are focused on driving efficiency and increasing margin. But there will also be non-financial benefits too. For example, providing your people with improved processes and systems to make doing their jobs easier or creating a more seamless interaction with your teams for suppliers and customers.

The combination of financial and non-financial benefits is very powerful; both need to be defined at the outset – not just so that you can celebrate success when you achieve them, but it helps inform the narrative as to why you are doing this. It gives people an understanding of what's in it for them and how it will feel when the work is done.

## Design out complexity

Wherever you are on the change spectrum, and whatever your risk appetite, modifying your operating model must be underpinned by a fundamental design principle: always seek simplicity and drive out complexity.

Removing degrees of complexity is essential to improve efficiency. Focusing your efforts on this principle will help you better answer design questions such as:

- What are your core processes and how can they be improved?
- What processes are adding little or no value?
- Where and how are people deployed in the organization – are there too many or too few?
- Where are bottlenecks or inefficiencies being experienced from the perspective of the employees, managers and – most importantly – customers?
- What are the key metrics measuring the efficiency of the organization?

It is inevitable that as an organization grows, complexity inadvertently gets embedded as things get bolted on to existing ways of working. But understanding the answers to these questions in order to drive out complexity should be at the heart of your quest for better, faster, cheaper ways of doing things.

The other common mistake that occurs is designing for exceptions. Too often, people worry about how exceptions will be managed, and this becomes a driving force that increases complexity. Whereas a quest for simplicity should focus on making the route that works more than 90 percent of the time as frictionless as possible, whilst noting the exceptions and having a way to manage those as just that: exceptions.

So, the key to any operating model modification is to ensure it does exactly what you want – removing complexity and increasing efficiency. Before you implement any changes, you can reduce your risk by running a trial or pilot. This will enable you to test scenarios to ensure that the to-be state is sound and there are no unintended consequences. Adding this step might feel like it will slow you down, but ultimately it will ensure that the changes that do get implemented stick.

## Case study: Designing out complexity

A logistics organization had a central portal, which was a repository for key operational documents and information for their front-line staff. This had been originally created for a singular purpose, but over time, multiple different things had been dumped into the portal without any thought as to how the information was organized or structured.

Worse still, the names of the documents and links to them that staff had to choose from had been designed by those who authored them. They were largely numeric in nature, reflecting a process or a part of the business which went by that name for those working within the corporate centre, but were largely meaningless to those accessing the information.

It had been this way for so long that front-line staff had given up complaining about it, accepting the fact that this was simply the way it would always be. But this had not lessened the frustration and had incrementally built inefficiency into the way in which the operation worked, due to the amount of lost time searching for key information, which increased both direct and indirect costs. All of this resulted in delays in staff being able to move things in a timely way for the customer.

Discussions with the end users of the portal quickly established the most important and frequently accessed information. This was then organized into logical groups and the portal was re-designed so that the user could click on one button to take them to all the relevant information they needed in that category. Documentation was re-named with the end user in mind. And extraneous information was moved elsewhere.

Taking something that had become complex over time and making it simple removed frustrations, improved morale, drove efficiency and ultimately saved the company hundreds of thousands of pounds a year. The organization ran the new and old systems alongside each other to allow for change adoption and uptake by the workforce, which they expected to take around four weeks. However, as they had engaged end users in the root cause identification of the issues and the design of the new solution, they had produced something which was intuitive and easy to use, and soon found that no-one was accessing the old system in just ten days.

# Design in efficiency

The combination of understanding your core purpose and designing an operating model that works optimally in service of that is not easy. But for organizations that do achieve this, it creates a virtuous cycle that reaps huge rewards – especially when you use data to track and drive continuous improvements.

One of the best examples of a virtuous cycle is at Amazon, where lower prices lead to more customer visits. More customers increase the volume of sales and attracts more commission-paying third-party sellers, allowing Amazon to get more out of their fixed costs. Underpinned by highly optimized lean processes, this efficiency then enables Amazon to lower prices even further.

The Amazon virtuous cycle is an example of the Jim Collins flywheel effect. Jim Collins wrote the seminal book *Good to Great*,[1] which is referenced in various places in this book. Collins analysed the common themes that were adopted by organizations that made the leap from good to great. And one of these was the flywheel effect:

> 'In building a great company or social sector enterprise there is no single defining action, no grand program, one killer innovation, no solitary lucky break, no miracle moment. Rather, the process resembles pushing a giant heavy flywheel, turn upon turn, building momentum until a point of breakthrough, and beyond.'

In modifying your operating model, the core objective must be to make it more efficient. And measuring and monitoring the effectiveness of this demands data. In an ideal world this data would already exist, but in our experience, more often than not, it doesn't. As a result you will need to establish ways of generating and monitoring the data required. This must be done in service of the core objective – to show that you are delivering an improvement in the efficiency of the organization.

However, remember your new operating model may demand completely different data and management information to that which you previously collected. We have lost count of the number of times we have seen organizations with processes, systems and people all collecting data and information that is no longer needed or used to manage the business. So don't be afraid to stop things that are making you inefficient. Breaking this sort of cycle is often difficult as it can span different departments, processes and systems, but it is worth doing.

---

[1] J. Collins, *Good to Great*, First Edition, Random House Business, 4 October, 2001.

# Make the right technology choices (if required)

One of the most common ways that people modify their operating model is by the introduction of new technology – seeking to automate manual processes or implementing systems to manage repeatable tasks. These are often labelled digital transformations. This kind of change is generally pursued in the expectation that by deploying an IT system, improved efficiency will automatically follow, and fewer people will be required to do the work, increasing your margin.

These objectives are highly desirable but they don't emerge simply because the IT system has been replaced or upgraded. The system change is the *what* – it is a critical step in your morph from point A to point B. But people working in a different way – whether that be adopting new systems, processes or changing their behaviour – this is the *how*, and it is this which is critical to you if you are to realize the benefits of this change.

We've seen numerous examples of where this point has been missed. One which perfectly illustrates this is the roll out of a new Electronic Patient Record system in a major hospital. The case for this change was the very definition of a no brainer. Improved quality of care, improved patient experience, reduced risk of errors, and significant financial savings from needing to store and transport paper records. Clinicians and end users were engaged in the upfront selection of the system, and then the IT implementation team worked at getting it configured and live.

However, post the launch of the new system, the implementation team found themselves scratching their heads when they saw clinicians wandering around with pens in their hands, scribbling on scraps of paper, bewildered about why they weren't using the system. The simple fact was, they had failed to take the end users on the change journey, as they'd focused on the *what* and not the *how*. Without the *how*, the desired benefits were evaporating before their eyes.

So, if you believe that the deployment of new technology is critical to delivering your outcomes, first ensure you have clarity on the as-is and to-be state for your processes and, if you can, make those process changes without the use of technology. This allows you to see what benefits might be available to you before committing to the investment in technology. And the new processes also provide you with a robust set of requirements for any technology solution you choose to deploy.

# Pace of implementation

The reasons for modifying your operating model may vary, but whatever these are you need to have a plan and your ultimate control lever is the pace at which the change happens. This should be a conscious and considered choice, which supports the purpose and outcomes you need.

In this context it is worth considering where you need to position yourself on each of the continuums laid out below in a conscious and purposeful way, as this will determine the activities which you need to include in your plan.

How much time do you want or need to spend validating the as-is and to-be state, versus how much risk would there be for you to proceed on the basis of assumptions? Is it more important to get a Minimum Viable Product (MVP) out into the business quickly as a proof of concept or pilot that you can iterate from, versus needing the new way of working to be in its final perfect end state before you deploy it? And finally, where does the balance need to lie between instructing your employees to just do the new things, versus investing time in them owning and driving the solutions?

We have seen change programmes implemented at the faster end of the spectrum, where the plan is delivered based on a set of assumptions, a minimum viable product is released quickly into the organization, and people are simply instructed as to what the change is and what they need to do differently. This can be exhilarating for the people driving the changes, but tends to be a less positive experience for those on the receiving end. But there may be a very good contextual reason for doing this, such as the business being in distress and needing urgent action to survive, or driving post merger/acquisition integration to preserve value.

Wherever you position yourself on each of these axes, thinking about your choices is important for every one of the change levers:

- In our experience, some level of validation of your assumptions up front will save you more time than it occupies in your plan, as it will facilitate smoother and faster implementation. And if you validate with the end users of the changes you are planning to make, this gives you the opportunity to gain greater levels of ownership from your people, which will speed up change adoption.

- The Minimum Viable Product versus Perfection axis is a direct product of your risk appetite. On the one hand you don't want perfection to be the enemy of the very good in pursuit of your outcomes. But on the other hand there may be some core processes, such as invoicing or payroll, that you don't want to take any chances with at all.

- The position you take on the third axis is entirely a product of the culture you have or want to create. Undoubtedly, people owning the changes that are happening, where they understand the why, are educated on the what, and supported in the how, is by far the best position to take. But in cultures where levels of ownership are necessarily low, changes are small in scale or there is urgency behind the reason for change, then simple instructions may be sufficient.

Ultimately, if your plan is to be successful it needs to ensure the accurate identification of the root cause of the problem, enabling you to design a pragmatic and achievable solution, all delivered in a way which makes things stick.

The opposite of this is why so many operating model modification changes fail – root causes are not properly understood, so solutions don't address the issues and the ownership sits with the project team and not the people who need to embed these new ways of working.

Your context will drive where you sit on these three axes, how you construct your plan and the pace at which you deliver it. The important thing is to make them active, conscious choices and to revisit them periodically with the learning you get from doing.

# Communication – take your people with you

We've talked about processes and systems, which are two of the three core components of any operating model. But there is a third dimension – people. Any changes to processes and systems will inevitably have an impact on your people. The scale will be dependent on the significance of the changes you are making to your operating model. It could be as simple as a modification to a job description in terms of accountability or use of a new process, through to the need to fundamentally restructure roles to reflect significant changes.

Whatever change you are planning, taking your people with you is critical and this is where the influence side of the Map is vitally important. It starts with building a belief that the modification of the operating model will make their working experience better. Fundamentally, it is essential that you engender and encourage belief, positivity, commitment and ideas from the people who are impacted by the change.

The same requirement to engender belief matters even if you end up choosing to instruct your people, rather than take them on a journey where they fully own the changes. You want the same outcome. You want your people to believe that this is something which is good for them. Generating that belief will create an accelerant for progress, as it speeds up adoption and adherence to new ways of working.

Every component on the Morphology Map matters, but the communication element of the Map is the lynchpin for everything you do. You can never over communicate. Think about your working life – have you ever worked in an organization where people say there is too much or even enough communication? Or is it true that it is one of those areas that is constantly flagged by employees as needing work, whether that be about the channels used to communicate or the content?

As someone once said to us, only when you are bored of saying it have your audience started listening. We forget when we craft communication that when we say it, it is the first time people have heard it. We've spent hours, days or even weeks crafting the narrative, the language, and any supporting content such as guidance or frequently asked questions. We've lived it and breathed it trying to think of every possible angle or permutation. Then we say it once and expect people to get it straight away. When you put it like that you can see why it doesn't work.

The communication and engagement swim lane in your plan should be one long, constant bar which starts before and ends later than everything else. It needs to be properly resourced in terms of both content creation and delivery. There needs to be sufficient capacity created in the diaries of the leadership teams in your organization to be briefed on the communication, have time to understand it and get confident in both delivering it and handling any questions.

And most importantly of all, you should build in regular feedback loops to enable the plan to be adjusted to respond to that feedback and any resistance encountered. On the one hand, activities that generate high levels of ownership may mean adoption is quicker, and you can generate momentum with rolling waves of changes that enable a faster pace. On the other, if resistance is greater than expected, plans may need to be adjusted to invest more time and energy in reducing this, placing a temporary brake on pace and progress.

---

## Case study: Take your people with you

A large public sector organization was undergoing a major transformation programme that encompassed all aspects of their operating model. The programme was designed to change the way in which staff were organized, the way they worked, the way their performance was measured and rewarded – all underpinned by the introduction of new technology.

Fundamentally the transformation programme was driven by a need to make the organization more efficient in delivering to its end customer, and core to this was bringing in industry best practice ways of working.

However, the emotional impact of this programme of change on staff was profoundly significant and it was understandably met with significant resistance. The case for change at a macro level was understood by all. However, the case for change at an individual level was less obvious and the links to the macro argument weren't clear, making it hard for people to see what was in it for them. This was particularly true amongst the staff who had been with the organization for several years.

To overcome this resistance a Change Advocate Network was established. The network set out to attract those members of staff who could see the benefits of the proposed changes to them, in terms of working more efficiently and enhanced career development opportunities. These advocates were supported by the provision of information and events that were designed to help them articulate the benefits of the transformation programme, and equally for them to feedback their own concerns and frustrations.

As a result the network grew rapidly, driven by the day-to-day interactions of the advocates who were able to explain to their colleagues the positive impact of the changes being implemented, and how they would improve their day-to-day working environment. It brought the changes being implemented to life and encouraged those who were unconvinced to discuss their concerns.

This increase in membership of the network and its associated feedback was critical to the overall communication elements of the plan and began to influence a faster overall delivery pace.

# Communicate your progress

Do remember to consider human nature when you are celebrating success. People have a natural tendency to point out things that are wrong and quickly forget when things have been improved. In a recent whole organization turnaround, when dozens of pain points had been identified, people needed to be constantly reminded of the improvements that had been made.

This was frustrating for the programme team who had gone out, listened to front line staff and designed the various projects around their feedback. When they went out as part of their regular engagement, they would get continued complaints about the things yet to be tackled but no acknowledgement of the work delivered to date. In response, the programme team would gently ask: how are things with issue A or issue B now, and then see people recall that yes, those changes had actually made their life better. They'd just moved on already to the next thing that they wanted to be addressed and needed reminding of the progress already made.

This is one of the many reasons why celebrating your progress is so important. It's like that top tip when creating presentations – tell them what you are going to say, say it, and remind them what you told them. It's the same with celebrating outcomes in change programmes. You start out saying why you are going to do something, you do it, and you need to say that it has been done. And that rhythm applies repeatedly throughout the changes. You don't do those things once, you repeat why, what you've done and the impact multiple times over the course of the change, creating an energy and momentum from celebrating success repeatedly as you work through the scope.

Doing this iteratively facilitates the ability to share and celebrate the compound effect of the changes that have been delivered. Communicating these results honestly and openly also has a number of positive effects:

- It reinforces the need for the change identified at the outset.
- It engenders greater commitment from the organization and encourages adoption of the target operating model.
- It creates a level of trust and confidence in those initiating and leading the change and makes it easier when further iterations are required.

The latter point is important. The need to morph is a constant if you are to survive or thrive, but you need to be mindful of the impact of change fatigue. Consider each time you morph as a wave of change that creates a new foundation for the next one. Morph, let those changes settle, look over your shoulder at how far you've come, celebrate that achievement, then morph again.

## BITE SIZE MORPHOLOGY
### Modifying your operating model

1. If you want to increase efficiency and clarity of purpose, modifying your operating model is a good choice.

2. If you have pulled the product or service diversification or merger and/or acquisition lever, you will need to review your operating model.

3. Tips for navigating this Morphology Map:

   · Any change must be in service of your core purpose – it engenders belief and support.

   · Minimize complexity and maximize efficiency.

   · Implement at a pace that matches the level of risk you are prepared to take.

   · Communication and influencing is a constant – you must take your people with you.

   · Seek feedback, listen and iterate your plan – it will drive the pace of adoption.

   · Communicate regularly and celebrate the progress you have made.

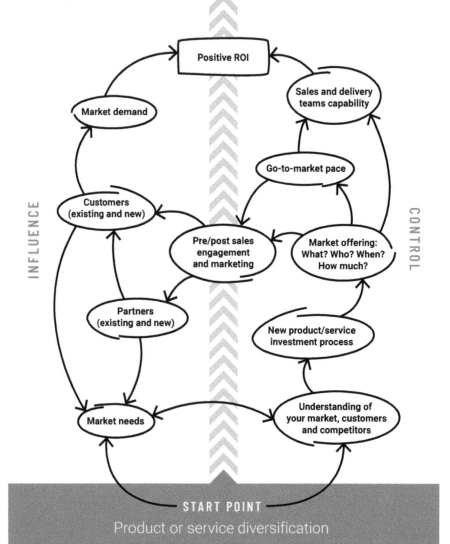

DESIRED OUTCOMES
· Different markets      · Increased revenue/profit
· Client retention       · New client attraction

Positive ROI

Market demand

Sales and delivery
teams capability

Go-to-market pace

INFLUENCE

Customers
(existing and new)

Pre/post sales
engagement
and marketing

Market offering:
What? Who? When?
How much?

CONTROL

Partners
(existing and new)

New product/service
investment process

Market needs

Understanding of
your market, customers
and competitors

START POINT
Product or service diversification

# Chapter 3
# Product or service diversification

*Wonder what your customer really wants? Ask, don't tell.*

Lisa Stone, CEO of Blogher

## Introduction

All products and services have a natural lifecycle:

- idea generation
- concept development
- market testing
- launch
- growth
- maturity
- decline

This lifecycle will vary in time between market sectors, but successful organizations have a portfolio of products and services that are coherent over time: as one product or service declines, another enters its growth or maturity phase. You also want to minimize the time from idea generation to product or service launch, while extending the amount of time spent in the growth and maturity stages of the lifecycle.

So, the life blood of a sustainable, growing business is the development of a steady stream of new products or services – enabling you to retain key customers, take a bigger share of your existing market, or enter new markets. You should always be thinking about opportunities to develop new products or services. The alternative is standing still, which risks a slow decline as you lose market share to your competitors.

But the successful generation and launch of new products and services is not straightforward. It requires an entrepreneurial flair that identifies a gap in the market in which you are operating or seizes on the introduction of new technology or ideas to create a new market need.

## Know your market, know your buyer

It sounds obvious doesn't it – before you launch a new product or service, you should ensure that you have as much understanding of your market as possible. Yet it is continually surprising to us how often blind faith, ego or over confidence sees investment choices on new offerings being made on the flimsiest of data. Of course, you can't know everything, and everyone points to innovators like Steve Jobs who created products no-one even thought they needed. But the market related elements on both the influence and control side of this Morphology Map are vital starting points for your plan.

Putting yourself in your customer's shoes so that you truly understand why they buy is vital to successful new product or service development. These motivations are complex but are usually driven by a number of factors which are well understood and exploited by most marketeers and sales organizations. As Lisa Stone says, there is no substitute for asking your customers in terms of gathering the best possible insight into why they buy, and what they want and need.

The approach of putting yourself in the shoes of the buyer is often known as user-led design in the technology sector, but it applies universally. How do customers behave? What are their challenges? What are their pain points that your offer could remove for them? This kind of insight is much broader than market data. It helps identify risks and wider market characteristics which turns it from data into truly useful information.

We worked with one organization where their services targeted a specific part of a business. But by truly understanding their customer needs they recognized that the drive to buy was never going to come from that part of the business. The pain point to be mitigated was cost reduction, which was absolutely the preserve of the finance directors.

Identifying that this group was the real buyer gave them a much more effective route to market. But that insight also meant the way they approached the delivery of their service took into consideration the threat they posed to the part of the organization they would be working with. This meant that they designed their delivery approach to help them succeed with their goals too.

This example perfectly illustrates the fact that to be successful in the launch of a new product or service you must see something different or know your customers better than everyone else. A transactional relationship, simply driven by cost, indicates you are a long way from understanding what motivates the true decision makers in your customer's organization. At the other end of this spectrum, professional service companies pride themselves on being present in the boardroom and influencing the decisions that define an organization's future direction. This enables them to tailor and pitch their services in a way that makes them invaluable to the success of any new venture. It also enables them to charge a premium for their services.

However you choose to approach it, it is essential to spend time and effort understanding your customers. This isn't something that is a one-off activity. It should be part of your operating model, so that it becomes a natural and iterative process that builds knowledge and confidence between both parties over time. It may take several months, if not years, but it should enable you to clearly articulate what your customer challenges or needs are at any given moment in time. Not taking the time to do this means you will be missing out on vital insight which should inform any new product or service you are developing.

## Know your competition

Understanding your market isn't solely about insight on what customer needs are or the problems you might be able to solve. It is also about being aware of what your competition is up to. They may be taking the market in a new direction, or they may have the scale and means to move at a faster pace than you, even though you might create the initial opportunity.

Being aware of what your competitors are doing is a vital part of your plan. And it needs to be continually revisited. Your own diversification will alter the marketplace. If competitors see you fulfilling a demand which they can offer too, they may copy your product and service like for like. Or they may do it in a way which has more features or a different price point, which will then require you to respond.

# Case study: The impact of not understanding your buyer and your competition

An independent provider of advanced technology solutions in the physical security market positioned themselves so that they could solve problems for customers that they didn't realize they had. They realized that the deployment of integrated security products could be a game changer for large scale public events that only occurred infrequently – a single adaptable solution to meet all the needs of a customer.

The offering was based on a concept of using best of breed technology (CCTV, remote detection assets, facial recognition) that could be rapidly configured and integrated together to provide the security commander with a real-time picture of what was going on, and where potential threats were likely to emerge.

Although the use of this approach is entirely standard now, it was ground-breaking at the time and supported by security practitioners who knew how difficult it was to secure and manage infrequent large-scale public events. However, these security practitioners were not the buyer, they were part of the end-user community. And as can often be the case with ground-breaking new services, it suffered from a number of unforeseen challenges.

The selling point of the integrated technology solution was based upon saving money for the end customer by needing fewer people.

But ultimately, the buyer of this new solution was the organization handling security on behalf of the end customer, and this undermined their business model which relied on the deployment of large numbers of people. There was also an emotional angle to the motivation of buyers, as fewer visible security people reduced the public's sense of feeling secure and being protected.

The second major problem was the timing of this solution. At the time, each of the best of breed systems were just that – best of breed – and, as a consequence, they were expensive and worked largely autonomously requiring significant effort (and cost) to integrate them. This increased the pricing and made the economic argument difficult to balance against the more standard approach of simply deploying more people.

The third major problem was the pace at which their competitors could react. Having identified the gap in the market, the large-scale technology providers – who were providing the best of breed systems – quickly responded and started to integrate their systems together to offer security providers and end customers customizable solutions that were cheaper, more advanced and integrated together seamlessly.

The lessons were there for all to see. Having identified a need, the business hadn't spent enough time understanding who the ultimate buyer of the solution would be. Equally they had underestimated the speed with which their competitors, who had much deeper pockets, could replicate and enhance the solution – thereby increasing their own revenues on the back of a competitor's idea, while pricing out a new entrant.

The overall result? Only a few customers purchased their first-to-market solution and those that did migrated to off-the-shelf options very quickly. This resulted in the independent provider withdrawing from the market and incurring significant development costs that could never be recouped.

# You need a process

Whether you are a start-up or a multi-national with a huge research and development budget, the development of a new product or service and the accompanying investment decision needs to be supported by a process, which should be at the heart of your plan. Usually when you hear the word process it implies bureaucracy, but that is very definitely not what we mean. When we use the word process, we are talking about a framework that allows you to evaluate your options, test it with the market, and iterate based on feedback. It should be dynamic and enabling. This new product or service development process also needs to lay out the criteria for progressing from one stage to another, as you iterate towards the launch of your new product or service. Adopting a stage-gate process will ensure that decisions on whether to continue or not are made objectively and independently, at the right time.

The process you put in place will be dependent on the type of organization you are, your risk appetite and the outcomes you want. But there are some consistent steps that you would want your process to include:

1. Evidence that a market exists for your idea: all kinds of data can feed into this, but some kind of primary research is a must to be able to avoid being seduced by beguiling hypotheses or untested assumptions. Areas for validation could include:

   - Is there genuine demand in the market?

   - What is the potential size and shape of the demand?

   - What geographies or territories is this limited to?

   - Are there signs already of a pull from the market for this offer?

   - How mature is the market and, therefore, how open to competitive forces might this venture be?

   - What are your existing customers telling you they want or need from you?

2. The analysis from this should inform the criteria in your evaluation process. Where there is more than one choice, this will help you establish which options should be a priority to pursue based on your competitor and broader market

assessment, including timelines, access and scale. It should also identify any regulatory or compliance factors which might be relevant to your offer. Ultimately if you don't have evidence that your existing customers have a significant problem that your solution can fix or that prospective customers are expressing a strong desire for something that your solution will address, then you should stop here. If the technology provider in the case study about the security market had done this objectively they may have saved themselves significant amounts of time and money.

3. Strategic alignment: you need to be sure that pursuing this market supports your overall strategy or broader business direction and that you have what it takes to win in this market. This question is an easier one to answer if you are extending an existing product or service within your current market or customer base, as you will have confidence in the capabilities you need to win new business in this area. If you are branching out into entirely new products, services or markets then this will inevitably be a judgement call, but you should still try and test those assumptions. Speaking to others who've tried the market before – learning from organizations who have both succeeded and failed – can help deepen your understanding of what it will take to win.

4. Quality of proposition design: can you (and have you) designed a proposition that resonates with the market? Again, the more primary data you can gather here by testing the offer with potential customers for the product and service, the more you will enhance your chances of success and minimize the need for subsequent iteration, or even full-scale re-design.

5. Test, learn and iterate: once you have passed those first four validation steps, your process should move into a cyclical and iterative phase where you are constantly evaluating your progress against the following key questions:

   • Can you successfully deliver against this proposition? Are you delivering the value that you promised to your customer?

   • Can you acquire new customers on the back of this proposition?

- Can you continue to improve both of these to reach your target number of customers, profitability and overall return on investment you are looking to achieve?

# Funding and return on investment

The steps above will, of course, get you to a point where you believe your new product or service is viable from a market perspective. But the other component of any evaluation process needs to be focussed on the financial implications of the decisions you are making. At the start of the overall process it is not uncommon for the funding required for development of a new service or product to be broad. But, as you iterate, the costings need to become more and more accurate, enabling you to consider the end-to-end financial resource required to launch your new product or service. This should include not only the product or service development time and effort, but also take into consideration the sales and marketing budget and the resources needed to deliver and support the products and services over time.

However you choose to fund it – from your balance sheet or through external investment – there needs to be clear criteria that are met before any further development takes place. In most cases, the level of investment in cash, time and effort for any new product or service development means that you will require sign off from the top of your organization to carry on. The fewer number of layers there are between whoever is leading on the work and the executive team or the board, the better in terms of supporting dynamic and proportionate governance.

So, setting clear criteria for continuation or further investment is critical. Clearly, if the demand for a new product or service is insufficient to warrant the cost of further development the decision to stop is clear cut. However, if you do proceed through to a full scale launch you should have a view on the return you are expecting not just at that point, but also further through the life cycle of the product or service. How is the return on investment looking after one, two and three years? What has been the cost of acquiring those customers and how do you use that data to pivot or persevere?

Your organization's context and the industry sector will set the risk appetite for how long you are prepared to let a new offer stay in the pre-revenue stage. Remember, you are in control of the pace of the product or service development you are driving, but you are not in control of the pace of adoption, you can only seek to influence that.

# Case study: The value of validating assumptions with evidence

A large telecoms organization with strong brand recognition believed that they needed to develop and launch sub-brands with their own unique identities. Their rationale was that it would allow them to target a younger customer demographic, enabling them to improve their overall market penetration and market share in a highly competitive sector.

Having settled on this strategic direction, they used a mix of external agencies to test the market. All were briefed on the target demographic and were asked to return primary data, together with analysis and insight on what this particular market segment wanted and needed from their mobile provider. The choice to use different agencies was deliberate, to avoid the reliance on any one organization and any bias that might exist within their sample group.

When the research phase was completed, there was then a level of triangulation across the findings to hone in on the common themes where there were multiple sources of evidence to support them. This highlighted that the needs and wants of their target customers were a combination of the tangible and emotional: contract flexibility, more data and a straight-talking provider.

The product development team moved quickly to design a proof of concept offer that would meet those needs. This covered the core product itself, the brand that would be wrapped around it and the tone of voice and visuals that would resonate with their target customers. Crucially, the primary research had highlighted the combination of these things would be critical to success – the product need to be supported by the brand, and vice versa. Just doing one wouldn't work.

The new brand and service offer was launched in the market within six months. Again, the primary research had enabled the organization to focus on only on those requirements customers had said they would need to see immediately to form a judgement in the development process. These were seeing the packages, being able to easily pick one (and switch between them if they wanted to) and get access to the service quickly. By focusing on those areas that they knew their potential customers would need, it ensured they didn't waste time considering features that they had previously scoped but now knew wouldn't matter, for example, instant cancellation options or family packages. All nice ideas, but not needed for this target market.

As soon as the service offer was launched, they quickly moved their attention to two things. First, driving customer acquisition as fast as possible by rapidly iterating their marketing approach based on learning from those areas that generated the highest number of new customers. And second, relentlessly focusing on the quality of the service provided by speaking weekly to brand new customers to understand their needs and where they could improve the service – effectively continuing their primary research when the offer was live in the market.

The time and investment in validating assumptions with primary research meant that they could focus their development effort on the key features that mattered and could confidently take the service to market within six months. They had exceeded all the targets that they had set for themselves within six months of the service being launched and their first sub-brand had become the UK's highest rated mobile network on Trustpilot.

## Market offering

The output of your development process will be a clear understanding of what your market offering will be. Fundamentally it will define the scope of the product or service you are going to launch, who the target customers will be, when you are able to start selling and how much will it sell for. Much of this information is critical to your launch programme and your pre- and post-sales engagement activities.

At this point these parameters are also entirely within your gift. In terms of the scope of your product or service the Minimum Viable Product (MVP) principle that we talked about in the previous chapter is a digital concept which applies just as well to other types of products or services. Getting something into the hands of customers which addresses their immediate needs is the fastest way to start to get feedback and insight on the best ways to either reach more customers with the same offer or adapt the product or service by the addition of new features. Think of this as a pilot that you build on over time.

Your willingness to go to market with an MVP is entirely down to a combination of your risk appetite and the competitor threat that you identify in your market analysis. You don't want to take something to market that a business with more scale and resources can copy and build on in a faster time. There are lots of examples of this in history where better products were overtaken by alternatives which reached market saturation sooner such as VHS versus Betamax or Apple versus Android.

Another key component of any new product or service is its differentiation – why does your new product and service look more attractive to existing and new customers in your chosen markets? This can be as simple as innovation with a small 'i'. It could be repackaging, a product or service extension or a different pricing strategy. Whatever you choose, it should be centred on creating something that is new and differentiated in the eyes of your customer.

This sort of innovation is inherently iterative. And the type of product or service will determine the frequency of that iteration. For example, digital products will iterate faster than offline solutions – but they all need to iterate based on feedback from the market. However good your new product or service development process is, you won't get it right first time. You should ensure that your plan includes regular feedback loops from customers – from those who buy and those who don't.

And, of course, the price of your new product or service is vitally important. Although this is completely in your control at the outset, you should be prepared to change tack rapidly. Your sales team are a useful source of knowledge to inform pricing strategies. But when you are taking something completely new to market no-one knows how much it is worth. Which means your starting price position is as likely to be about how much value the customer sees in the offer, rather than how much it costs you to deliver it.

That value point is especially important if the offer contains intellectual property (IP) which is unique to you. Too often businesses focus on protecting their IP but don't think about how they might be able to use it as a premium for their price point, missing an opportunity to go beyond the recovery of sunk costs when taking a new offer to market.

Getting this right is not easy. You need to price your product or service so that the customer perceives it as attractive in terms of the value and benefit it provides to them. This may mean cost recovery is delayed in the initial phase of market adoption, but the alternative is a product that is sitting on a shelf unsold or a service that is not being delivered at all.

Much of the above is concerned with the *what* of your market offering but there also needs to be a consideration of *how*. For example, can partnering or white label solutions help you get to market faster, especially where competitor threats are high? We've seen service organizations partner with technology providers to put a new service wrap around their products. That helped the technology provider extend the life cycle of their product and use the service provider as a feedback loop from customers for future product development. And it allowed the service provider to create a new revenue stream with very low levels of investment in an area where they didn't have strong internal capabilities.

And don't forget to think about how to protect your new product or service. What do you need to put in place in respect of controls or patents to restrict others from copying or replicating it under a different brand? This can be a lengthy and expensive business so if you this applies to you, then start early and seek expert advice.

# Pre/post sales engagement and marketing

We started out by saying you need to understand your market, customers and competitors and if you do this in an interactive way rather than desk research, then you have effectively started your pre-sales engagement and marketing. Every conversation you have with a current or potential customer all counts.

You need to be thoughtful about both your timing and who you approach in this activity. At the outset you'll need high degrees of trust in those you engage with to protect any competitive advantage in the early phases of refining the offer. Whereas you may be more relaxed about wider audiences later in the process when you are looking for bigger volumes of validation for your offer, and the bulk of the work has been done making it harder for a competitor to steal a march on your launch.

Whilst it is externally focused, this is no different to the communication and engagement activities for internal changes. It starts early and needs to be a continual focus throughout to gather feedback that enables you to iterate along the way. Every conversation will help triangulate data, validate assumptions and inform the formal go-to-market plan which is where your pre- and post-sales communication and engagement really kicks in. These activities are firmly focused on the Influence side of the Map.

Your objective is to reach customers (existing and new) and persuade them that they need your new product or service. You can, of course, do this yourself, particularly by the exploitation of social media but you will inevitably need more horsepower in this part of your plan. What that looks like will depend on the offer you are taking to market, but might include marketing agencies, lead generation companies, social media campaigns and more. And never forget the simple truth that people buy from people and trust underpins those choices. Every person in your organization is an advocate and a salesperson. Make sure they have enough information to be promoting the offer in every interaction they have, whether that be inside or outside of work.

# Go to market planning

Having a plan is the singular theme of this book, but we cannot emphasize the importance of this part of the new product or service process enough. Too often, product or service diversification focuses on idea generation and concept development, and neglects the go to market planning and any in-service support required post sale. Inevitably, organizations that ignore these vital issues tend to fall foul of the build it and they will come fallacy. Every successful new product or service launch has to be underpinned by a clear go to market plan.

It starts by building on the market analysis phase, which should have highlighted where you can get to market fastest – usually this is where there is a recognized market that already exists, and you have the capabilities to exploit it.

Once you know where and who, you can build a rigorous campaign to take the offer out to your potential customers. This should start with the recognition that its primary purpose is to help get customers past the barrier of being one of the first to say yes. Remember, even if your analysis has identified that a problem exists in your market, your customers might not yet be ready to take on the solution.

One of the best ways to overcome this is to target existing or warm customers who trust you and are willing to take the time and energy to try something new to give them a competitive advantage. You may even incentivise these early adopters with a reduced price to gain traction in the market. The beauty of this approach is it provides you with real evidence of the associated benefits of using the new product or service, as well as reference sites which might be the tipping point for other customers to also be persuaded to try something new. It also gives you the opportunity to test that your post-sales support capability is delivering excellent service.

You must be realistic about the time it takes to get that traction in any new market. In our experience, moving from a new offer to a consolidated position with a reliable income stream takes time, and is entirely dependent on the industry sector and context.

As a planning guide, in the services sector, you may get there as quickly as three to four months if you have strong existing industry knowledge or expertise which you can package up in a targeted way. Alternatively, it could take as long as 18 months or more if your solution is novel, or you need to acquire and develop new people capabilities to deliver it. Pilots are a useful tool to try and shorten the go to market life cycle, but your biggest determinants of pace are the depth of your financial backing and having the specific capabilities within your team to move quickly.

For new products, if you do not have something in customers' hands which is generating revenue within a year, you are probably too slow. But having an established product presence can take as long as three to five years.

Although the above timelines are a useful rule of thumb you may get lucky due to emerging market or environmental changes. Some products might have low or moderate success to start with, but a context change occurs which they can capitalize on. The COVID-19 pandemic provided countless examples of this. The rise of video conferencing technology and the use of Zoom to address the need for home working is a prime example. In healthcare, the technologies and services behind Test and Trace not only generated increased revenue streams, but also the scale and means to further invest in new products and services at a faster rate than would have been possible without that explosion of growth. Similarly, in less obvious markets like online horticultural businesses, their previously steady organic growth then took off as people spent more time at home tending gardens.

# Building capability

Assuming your market insights are sound, and your process has ensured that you prioritize the right products or services, your sales engine becomes one of your critical success factors. Your plan should ensure there is sufficient time to educate your sales force on the new product or service. Remember that confidence in sales teams tends to come from selling what they know well.

A new product or service offer needs a new set of capabilities within your sales team. As well as investing in training on the new offer, and the potential sales hooks identified from your market insight, it is also critical to involve your sales team in the development of the associated marketing collateral. This helps them understand how to engage in conversations with potential customers about how it would solve their problem. It also allows them to be thoughtful about potential targets who they know this will resonate with, which is likely to get more traction than a scattergun sales approach where the whole salesforce talks to everyone about the new offer, regardless of relevance.

The other critical area to concentrate on is delivery. Having sold something new, be it a product or a service, your organization must be ready to deliver on the promises made to your customers. This could well require you to modify your operating model in a number of different ways. It could mean anything from re-organizing teams and training service desk operators, through to setting up a new delivery team in a new geography. Other things that will need attention are supply chain considerations:

- How dependent are you on your supply chain for the new product or service to succeed – whether on a component basis or wholesale supply of services?
- How resilient and reliable is this supply chain?
- What would happen if this resilience were to reduce?

This analysis of the supply chain might even cause you to consider the merger or acquisition change lever, in order to manage that risk by securing the capabilities you need to succeed on a permanent basis.

Having sold your new product or service, the post sales customer experience is what differentiates one business from another. And it is your people who hold the key to that experience. You must take your people on this journey through the highs and lows of taking a new product or service to market. You will require high degrees of trust, honesty and transparency to make sure that all the energy you put into creating and launching your new product or service is successful.

And a footnote on the engagement and capability building of your sales and delivery team – as we said earlier, don't forget that everyone in your organization is a salesperson who might be able to open doors for you. Whether that is a member of your delivery team, or just the wider professional and personal networks where people can share information about the offer. Make sure you equip everyone to create sales opportunities for you.

# Case study: A glorious innovation failure – how not to do it

A large organization wanted to increase its service offer to the small business sector. The leadership team had identified it as an under-served niche where customer experience was anecdotally poor. They could see disruptor brands emerging in their sector and wanted to ensure that they weren't left behind.

They engaged an agency to undertake some analysis to try and understand what the customer problems were, and how they could turn them into opportunities for new product or service development. One particular pain point was highlighted from this research and a small innovation unit, comprising of fewer than ten people, was established to see how they might alleviate that pain point with a rapid roll out of a new app. The app was designed to give free value to the target customers, but ultimately serve as an acquisition tool for follow-on revenue generating products and services.

Within a year the innovation unit had risen to around 80 people, bringing in a range of external capabilities from agencies and the contractor market. But they still hadn't delivered the promised new app to solve the customer problem. One of the leadership team was moved on for challenging whether they really had established a market need, and the team were instructed to get on with the app development and deliver the features that had been agreed months ago.

They ended up making an acquisition to secure the capabilities they needed to complete the app, which was finally released after 18 months. But the unit was shut down after another year and no outputs from the two and a half years they had been in existence ever realized a return on that investment for the organization. Sign-ups to the app were in the low thousands and a tiny number of customers had been upsold the additional service on the back of it. It had been a catastrophic failure – squandering an eight-figure investment sum for a negligible return.

The root cause of this failure was the over reliance on the initial research which only took four to six weeks and spoke to a handful of people. There was not enough depth in the market insight on which they could confidently build, and it took them almost two years to speak to another 10–15 potential customers. Their assumptions were untested, and the leadership insistence to just deliver had all the hubris of the 'build it and they will come' approach.

There was no reflection on the barriers to the pace of progress in that first 18 months, and the drive to deliver something over rode the necessity of solving customer problems. They didn't notice the stifling corporate governance that had been imposed with this separate innovation unit being subject to an approvals process which meant the pace of progress was blocked at every turn. And they didn't equip it with the right capabilities – only two of the ten-plus leadership team had any experience of taking new technology products to market and it wasn't a core capability anywhere else in the organization.

### BITE SIZE MORPHOLOGY
## Product or service diversification

1. A good idea is just that, if no one wants it.

2. Design and launch of a new product or service cannot be done in a vacuum.

3. Tips for navigating this Morphology Map:
   - Understand your market, your buyers and what your competitors are up to.
   - Have a process which enables you to make objective decisions and iterate.
   - Be able to articulate the offering to your market: features, benefits, price and value.
   - Engage existing and potential customers.
   - Have a robust go to market plan, with sales and delivery teams in place and ready.
   - Timing is everything, make sure your customers are ready and make sure you are too.

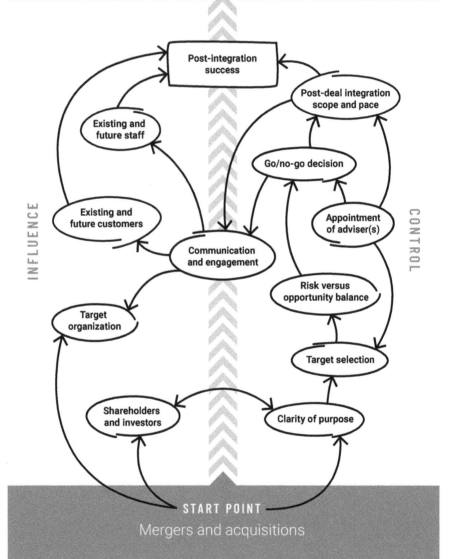

DESIRED OUTCOMES
• Increased market share  • Different clients/markets
• Increased resilience  • Increased revenue/profit

Post-integration success

Post-deal integration scope and pace

Existing and future staff

Go/no-go decision

Existing and future customers

Appointment of adviser(s)

INFLUENCE

CONTROL

Communication and engagement

Risk versus opportunity balance

Target organization

Target selection

Shareholders and investors

Clarity of purpose

START POINT
Mergers and acquisitions

# Chapter 4
# Mergers and acquisitions

*If opportunity doesn't knock, build a door.*

Milton Berle

## Introduction

On the face of it this lever can look like the option to move your business forward fastest. A big step forward rather than incremental, organically driven change. A quick fix for building resilience or acquiring market share and new routes to new opportunities. Or a doorway to a new future as Milton Berle suggests, above. But without doubt this is at the top of the risk scale and research indicates than around 80 percent of mergers or acquisitions (M&A) fail to deliver the value they set out to achieve.

The reasons for this high failure rate are varied, but include one or more of the following:

- unrealistic return on investment expectations
- flawed appreciation of markets
- stopping at the point the deal is done
- even when planned for, poor post-acquisition integration
- cultural clashes
- misaligned operational processes.

That shouldn't deter you from pursuing this option if it is the right strategic choice, but it should strengthen your resolve to ensure you develop a credible plan that enables you to avoid the pitfalls that beset undertakings of this nature. We've mentioned repeatedly the importance of responding to what you are learning and experiencing when implementing your plan, whilst remaining focused on the outcomes you want to achieve. When choosing this lever, that is more important than ever.

# Be clear on why

Evidence would suggest that serial acquirers are more successful than those who undertake an acquisition on an occasional basis.[2] This is because those who regularly undertake acquisitions have a well-oiled process in place that rigorously qualifies their acquisition targets based upon their strategic objectives. Typically, these objectives will be in service of increasing shareholder return and contain one or more of the following:

- increased market share
- access to new markets
- geographic expansion
- increasing revenues and/or margins
- response to competitor consolidation
- access to Intellectual Property or dormant assets
- removal of a competitor.

These are the fact-based reasons that will determine the style – friendly or hostile – of the acquiring organization and also the level of risk they are prepared to take. But mergers and acquisitions can also be driven by emotional factors:

- personal ego and ambition
- desire for recognition amongst peers
- excitement
- why not? We have lots of cash on the balance sheet!

In reality, the pursuit of a merger or acquisition strategy is a combination of both the factual and the emotional. It takes significant time and

---

[2] Hansell, Walker, and Kengelbach, *Lessons from Successful Serial Acquirers,* Boston Consulting Goup, 2014, www.bc

energy, coupled with a degree of courage. But that does not detract from the fact that if you are to be successful you need to be logical, objective and focused. And at the heart of this are a number of key questions: Why am I doing this? What am I seeking to attain? Why do I need it? And will the shareholders and investors support this? Don't just ask these questions at the start of the process – your plan should create the opportunity to revisit them regularly.

Common causes of failure in mergers and acquisitions are when emotion starts to override a rational process. Too often, people get caught up in the momentum created by a merger or acquisition, and this prevents them from recognizing that it might not work. Saying no is an acceptable position to take right up until you sign on the dotted line.

# Target selection

The fundamental reasons for pulling this lever must be for the target organization to add value. Often, the start point will centre on the financials: What are the cost savings that can be secured? What new revenue streams does it open up? What does it do to the top line and bottom line once achieved? Of course, these are crucial considerations but there are other equally valid issues that need to be considered:

- Do you have the managerial capability and capacity to enact the deal?
- Do you have the managerial capability and capacity to manage integration?
- How aligned to your core capability are the products and services you are acquiring?
- Is the target too big or too small?
- Does the target fit from a market perspective?
- Does the target fit from an organizational perspective?
- Does the target fit from a people perspective?
- Does the target fit from a cultural perspective?

And remember, the leaders of target organizations will have their own motivations, emotional drivers and imperatives. Due diligence will tell you a lot, but it won't tell you everything you need to know if you are to succeed with this change lever. Let's bring this to life through a case study.

# Case study: Right target, right outcome

After over 20 years of experience of working in IT transformation programmes across all sectors, an experienced IT Programme Manager decided to found their own consulting business. This was a partly driven by changes to the market with IR35 legislation, but it also created the opportunity to consider how they might have more control over their work. The decision was very much a lifestyle choice rather than a grow and exit strategy.

The business grew steadily over a five-year period based on word of mouth and the reputation the founder had established in the market, extending its reach across sectors and growing to employ over 25 people with a wider associate network. It had a clear purpose around becoming a trusted partner which always delivered for customers and had an unenviable track record of meeting every programme deliverable and target. All through a clear set of well bounded service specialisms. They knew what they were good at, and what they weren't.

They soon came to the attention of a global cloud and digital transformation services provider interested in acquiring them. They employed thousands of people across several worldwide locations, with a number of practice pillars spanning a much broader service offering. This business had grown with a strong customer focus and deep cultural identity which were values and people driven. These values were prominent in their marketing and how their people showed up every day.

Whilst the smaller consulting business had not been established with this kind of exit in mind, they were open to the approach and embarked on a series of bilateral discussions with two of the founders of the larger global practice. They eschewed formal due diligence and heads of terms, and instead conducted these initial discussions under a simple non-disclosure agreement. The reason for this?

They just wanted to get to know one another before initiating any formal process.

The founder of the smaller business described this as like dating – not rushing in and being sure before making a commitment. In reality, it was all about making sure the target selection was right – from both perspectives.

These discussions and informal meetings – including site visits, meeting teams and feedback from customers – allowed them to make a considered and well triangulated decision as to whether or not to proceed.

From the buyer's perspective they were able to truly understand the disciplines and skill sets they were acquiring and how they would support one or more of their established practices to grow across their markets. They understood how to best get the best out of the acquisition in terms of maintaining the consulting organization's brand, identity and reputation that had been so quickly established whilst still being able to extract value across the group.

From the seller's perspective, they had the time to consider how it would feel to be part of something bigger, how that might support sales opportunities for them and growth opportunities for their people, and gain assurance about maintaining their identity and levels of control.

And it gave both parties the chance to assess the culture of each organization. It built confidence in the personal drivers and motivations around the way they would deliver for their customers, and that the environment they created for their people was a good match.

It took half a dozen meetings over a couple of months to establish that the target selection was right and that enabled the formal process of acquisition and due diligence to be completed seamlessly in less than six weeks from start to finish, with the smoothest post integration plan we have ever seen.

> Spending time evaluating target selection isn't just the right thing to do to ensure you get value out of any transaction, it also saves time and money across all elements of your implementation plan.

# Opportunity and risk

Although undertaking a merger or acquisition represents a huge opportunity if you get it right, it does come with a degree of risk. Your entire approach to deploying this change lever will be driven by a combination of your risk appetite and your financial position which, together, form the backdrop to the strategic choices you make.

Where your financial reach is limited and you cannot use the resources on your own balance sheet to finance the deal, transferring equity in return for the finance required may mean you start to lose control of your business. You must be comfortable with what that means for you personally, as you move yourself into an environment where you will increasingly only be able to influence rather than control events directly.

At the outset of your plan, you have the greatest level of control and ability to reduce your risk. You can control the pace and timing of any activity and create the space for reflection and go/no go decision points. Your plan should not only focus on how you will achieve the transaction but, vitally, how you will operate when you get there. Completing the transaction is very much the start of the plan, not the end.

Failure to see this is the root cause of issues with the majority of transactions. It is absolutely essential that you take people with you and have a clear plan for your cultural aspirations. The structure of the deal may enable you to keep distinct cultures or demand that you create a new one. If you think of this through the lens of family units, you are effectively creating a step-family and asking people to move into someone else's house. It needs the same high degree of empathy and emotional intelligence to drive successful integration and understanding across the bigger organization. The People and Culture Morphology Maps can help you with this.

To help reduce your risk when pulling this lever there are three distinct groups of people you need to engage with and influence. You will need to work closely with your shareholders or the external investors supporting the transaction, as they enable the deal to take place. You will need to take the people from both organizations with you on this journey. And you will need to think about the customers and key suppliers to the two businesses, in order to maintain sales and the continued supply of your products or services. The timing of when you communicate and engage with each of these three groups varies and will be driven by a range of considerations, not least of which will be commercial confidentiality and the legal restrictions associated with the size and shape of the deal.

Whatever the timing of these activities in your plan, the commonality across all of these groups is the need to ensure they understand the logic underpinning why the transaction is taking place and engender within them the belief that the combined entity will truly be bigger, better and more capable of delivering improved outcomes for all.

# Get the right advice

Advisers are a necessary part of this process and, if chosen wisely, can be a critical part of ensuring that you look at the transaction in the round and increase the chances of success. As with many things in business, if this is new to you, you will likely turn to your network for recommendations.

One of the advantages of your investment in up-front thinking is that it enables you to ask for this support in a more nuanced way. Of course, you will need legal and financial advice, but depending on the scale of the transaction you may need support with the integration activities too. You should always seek advisers who will be rounded enough to understand the personal as well as practical dimensions – and remember, you need advisers both for the business but also yourself, as you might be asked to provide personal guarantees, or make decisions that affect your own financial position.

While advisers and due diligence are a necessary part of any transaction it is important to ensure that they don't overrun the process – everything needs to be proportionate and appropriate. Remember you are paying for these services, and you need to own and run the process, not them. Given that this isn't something that people do every day, it is easy to fall into a trap of being too deferential to advisers as they have the technical expertise. It's your transaction and they are providing a service to you. You set the scope, boundaries and approach. If you lack confidence on this point, your first adviser should be someone who has experience of doing this kind of thing multiple times so they can guide you, rather than the appointed advisers being able to take too much control.

We've seen transactions that get over-run by excessive and lengthy amounts of due diligence. This is usually because there is a degree of risk aversion within the buyer, but it comes at a cost implication for both parties. When you build your plan, build in conscious tolerance levels for how much time and effort you are prepared to spend on the different elements of the process. For example, if agreeing any initial heads of terms has been hard work before the due diligence starts, this is a warning sign for what is likely to be a lengthy and expensive process ahead.

# Go/no go

It is essential that you have the opportunity to make go/no go decisions at every stage in the process. And although most mergers and acquisitions tend to be predicated on the financial inputs and outcomes involved, these decision points shouldn't only be about the money. The landscape of advisers and other organizations who exist to support these transactions are skewed around the financial elements of any deal. We would challenge whether it is the financial dimensions that matter most.

Of course, it is important that the numbers make sense – paying the right price and funding the newly formed entity in order to generate further profits and sustainable growth in the future is a core objective. But if you think about this plan that narrowly, you will absolutely end up with post integration issues which may undermine all of the financial assumptions that you have focused on.

More often than not, the decision to pursue an acquisition or merger will hinge on a financial forecast which is underpinned by a set of assumptions which are almost always optimistic. For example, we can gain this turnover without the associated costs as we can collapse together support functions, or use existing infrastructure to deliver the higher volumes of products or services. Not only is that optimistic, it is also based on an assumption about the relative capabilities of your staff and those in the organization being merged with or acquired.

So yes, on one level you are buying revenue or profit. But what you are also buying is ideas, processes, products, services and, most importantly, customers and people. Because it is the customers that keep you in business and it is the people who deliver the products or services and make the organization tick. It is these two groups who deliver the value at the heart of your financial calculations and you should ensure you pay sufficient attention to understanding and then managing them well in your plan.

So, your go/no go decision needs to ensure that you are taking a rounded view of the transaction. It must mean you can confidently say yes to the following questions:

- I have fully explored all the strategic choices available; I know why we are doing this.
- The target organization aligns with our strategy.
- The deal has the full support of shareholders and investors.
- I've got the right advisers in place to support me, now and post deal.
- I've got an end-to-end implementation plan which covers the mechanics of the merger or acquisition, and a robust post transaction integration plan that fully embraces the people and cultural aspects of the new business.
- I've got the resources in place not only for the transaction, but also the post- merger/acquisition integration activities.
- I am confident that the markets in which we will operate, and the customers we have and will gain, can understand the logic of the deal and will find the service offering attractive.

- The financial return calculations have been fully analysed and there is a high level of confidence that they will be achieved.

Any gaps in the answers to these questions should make you pause and reflect – it is never too late to say no!

---

## Case study: Underestimating the impact of culture on successful post-acquisition integration

A specialist professional services business had grown very successfully over a five-year period. Founded by recognized experts in their field they had attracted some of the best and brightest talent in their sector to be part of a journey initially working in a small, high energy, entrepreneurial environment.

Their reputation for high quality delivery and functional expertise was their biggest asset, delivering tangible outcomes for their customers and thereby creating a natural sales pipeline through word of mouth, repeat business and recommendations. This, in turn, enabled them to attract more talented people who wanted to be part of a fast growing, innovative, disruptive brand in a commoditized marketplace.

There was a culture of genuine camaraderie, a sense that they were all part of something that mattered, and were in it together, which made people feel valued. It wasn't long before they found themselves as one of the fastest growing companies within their market and came to the attention of potential trade and investment acquirers.

This had always been the exit plan for the founders, and they were approached by a larger trade buyer with experience across various non-competing functional disciplines. In principle, this looked like a good fit – it would give them access to a much bigger sales pipeline and client lists for continued growth.

A significant due diligence period was conducted and the deal agreed. However, the reality was that the new parent company's culture could not be further removed from the business they had created. The acquiring organization centrally dictated the approach, with a focus on sales and revenue coming at all costs. And it wasn't long before the entrepreneurial founders recognized that they were in an environment which was everything they had created their own business to avoid. Worse still, they no longer had the control or decision-making ability to run and continue to grow the business in the way they had before.

Within 12 months from the point of acquisition, they had lost over half of their brightest talent and several of the founders had left the organization to progress other opportunities. Over time, further value was eroded from the business to leave it a shell of its former self. It was a salutary reminder that when acquiring businesses, cultural fit is paramount, and the capabilities which exist within the business itself is where the true value lies.

# The plan within the plan: post integration

The post integration plan element of the Map is where you either secure or destroy value. As the case study above describes, done badly, the value and benefits of pulling this lever can evaporate right before your eyes.

You can design the framework for this plan ahead of completing the deal, but a large part of the detail will need to be fleshed out once the transaction is done. This is because although due diligence will minimize your risk and increase your odds of success, it won't give you access to the finer details and nuances which you need to make your post-integration plan really deliver.

It's no different to any other major purchase. When you buy a house you view it more than once. You get a survey done. You might even go back to measure up for fixtures and fittings. You decide that you have chosen the best target for your requirements. You've done your due diligence. You've gathered enough information to prepare for the move. But then you move into the house and find that the door to the bathroom sticks, the floorboards on the landing are creaky, or there was an unexpected opportunity to convert the loft. You need to live in the place to understand those nuances, and it is no different when it comes to your integration plan.

## Integration plan, scope and pace

There is a school of thought that post-merger integration plans need to be executed quickly in order to preserve value for the acquirer, and reduce uncertainty for the people within both organizations. And to a degree, we have some sympathy for that perspective. Metaphorically tearing the plaster off quickly can be the right way to go. But we also believe that it is important that these activities follow the mantra of do it once and do it right. Get this wrong, and you've wasted your (or someone else's) money.

If you are to consider new organizational structures, operating model changes or consolidation of any infrastructure – be it physical, technological or data – it is wise to do so with a level of validation, rather than based on the assumptions made through due diligence and the transaction itself. You need to apply the same thinking and conscious choices that we set out in Chapter 2 across the three planning axes and strike the right balance between pace and risk mitigation. Especially when it comes to bringing people with you, who will naturally feel unsettled.

Key things to consider across the combined entity when you build your post-integration plan are:

- How will you evaluate the relative efficiency of the operating models?

- How will you evaluate the relative strengths and capabilities of individuals and teams?

- How will you understand the new customers and markets you have acquired?

- How will you learn about the reputation associated with the brand you have acquired?

- How will you assess the culture of the organization you have acquired?

The degree with which you need to do this is entirely dependent on the structure of the deal and how you envisage value being created. If this was an acquisition that will sit in a group structure and remain as you purchased it – common when taking out a competitor or acquiring market share – then your interest in making changes to how it operates on a day-to-day basis may be limited. But if you made the purchase to drive efficiency or margin improvement, or develop new capabilities, then it will pay dividends to focus on these questions early in order to inform your post-merger integration plan.

However long it takes you to execute the plan – whether you take time to validate or proceed on the basis of assumptions – constant, open, communication throughout is essential. The communication and engagement element of your post-integration plan is the most important one. Especially when it comes to retaining your best people, who are effectively the representation of the investment you have made. You don't need to have all the answers, but you do need to be transparent. It's okay to say you don't know the answer to a particular question yet. You might be able to say when you can answer it, you might not. Always start with reminding people why the transaction has happened, as this is the anchor point for all of your communication. Be open about what it means for people as soon as you practically can. And start to share what's in it for them once you can articulate it. And most of all, make them part of shaping the future, where it's appropriate.

# Being on the other side

The majority of the content in this chapter has focused on the motivations and activities relating to an acquisition or merger. There is, of course, the other side of the coin. What are the motivations and activities of those being acquired or as a minority player in a merger?

In reality, the Morphology Map is not that much different, but the prioritization and ability to control the process is reduced. The fundamental difference is the outcome. In our experience, the motivation to sell is driven by one or more of the following factors:

- need for shareholder return
- personal financial considerations
- market driven threats
- inability to grow
- loss of personal drive or motivation.

This is not an exhaustive list but, in our experience, anyone who is selling their business is not simply focused on a financial outcome. They want to see the business they have led to continue to thrive and for their staff and customers to have a strong future. As a consequence, anyone selling their business should try and ensure that a post transaction integration plan is in place and is as robust as possible. Of course, they may not be around to see it implemented, but most acquirers will insist on some kind of earn-out or transition period, as it is absolutely in the best interests of the seller to ensure that their staff and customers continue to be looked after in the future.

It is also important as a seller to recognize the emotional and personal impact of any sale or merger. It may be that you retain a position of authority in the new organization, providing you with new horizons and challenges. Or you may end up in a position where your sphere of influence, control and sense of ownership and motivation is diminished. For anyone who has led an organization for any length of time, selling is a significant step, and its emotional impact should not be underestimated.

## Case study: Always trust your instincts

Two entrepreneurial business managers with sales and accounting backgrounds, decided that a buy and build venture into another sector was their route to fame and fortune. They'd been part of successful management buy outs in their respective industries and wanted to put that experience to good use.

They invested £200k of their own money, and gave personal guarantees for a further £130k, in what was a highly leveraged deal to buy the first business: a litho printing company. The acquisition went well, and trading continued seamlessly. Profit forecasts were better than expected, so the debt was serviced and partially repaid. Twelve months in they purchased a second business, again focused on print production but with short-run digital printing and product finishing capability. The same experience followed, and post-acquisition integration worked well.

However, the first acquisition had one key fault line: a very dominant customer in its sales mix who accounted for over 75 percent of their revenue. This isn't unusual, but that carried a very significant risk. They had recognized this and the mitigation plan was to diversify and add more customers so that no one customer could account for more than 30 percent of total turnover.

As the old adage goes, life is the thing that gets in the way when you are busy making plans, and events soon overtook the owners, as the dominant customer announced a procurement review, the result of which was to significantly reduce the amount of work they gave to the first business they purchased.

As that was still a highly leveraged business, this decision meant they were now immediately in trouble, with profit turning to loss very quickly. The lost revenue was compounded by a high fixed cost base of printing machines and premises. Capacity utilization fell dramatically, and they were soon grappling with cash flow problems. Fortunately, the funders of the transaction remained supportive and believed in the talented management team to find a route out.

A new acquisition plan was developed. This time to buy a print management house with the belief that if they got the right one, it could win and direct work to production plants thereby restoring capacity utilization in the first acquisition on this buy and build adventure.

Huge effort went into finding targets at breakneck speed, and one was identified. The fact that it was already available for sale made their plan much easier to execute. Price negotiations were completed quickly as both seller and buyer were keen and heads of terms were agreed. The purchase price was the highest of the three acquisitions, so this further exacerbated the amount of debt on the balance sheet, but the management team were convinced it was the answer – think big, grow volumes through internal group trading as well as externally.

The due diligence went to plan, a great customer base was identified, and potential new income streams were welcomed – selling paper as well as print. The final negotiations started well but then began to just not feel right. It was difficult to quantify, but the management team knew it wasn't feeling right.

Lawyers, accountants, tax experts all did their bit to unearth risks, negotiate warranty and indemnity cover and disclosures against key risks. But still, something didn't feel right. What was it about this transaction? Completion day came and the lawyer advising the purchasers, very well known to one of them, asked the usual pre-completion question: are you sure you are comfortable with this transaction? Despite knowing that they weren't, as they couldn't quantify their concerns other than to say it was a gut feel, the purchasers completed the transaction.

Within a few days, the entire sales team of the newly acquired business walked out and set up in competition. The seller had always known that there was a high probability of this happening and hadn't disclosed it. There was nothing in the due diligence process that created any obligation for the staff making these threats to disclose their plans. Unbeknownst to the purchasers, there had been the equivalent of a stand-off taking place within the business they were acquiring. The seller never believed that the staff would walk out, while the staff were determined to do just that if the seller dared to sell the business.

Despite their instinct telling them that something didn't feel right, the purchaser proceeded with the transaction because they had convinced themselves that it was the dream ticket to resolve the under-utilization within other loss-making production facilities that they had acquired earlier on the journey. Deciding not to go ahead would have risked admitting failure in their whole buy and build strategy, but deciding to proceed brought it crashing down in a much more painful way.

The lessons from this story – always trust your instinct; never be afraid to walk away; and never try and buy your way out of trouble.

# Communication and engagement

As with all of the Morphology Maps, there is a large communication and engagement element to your plan for this lever. The size and scale of this change is arguably the most significant of all the change levers, and the communication and engagement activities need to be proportionately extensive. It has the widest range of audiences in respect of your own employees, customers, suppliers and shareholders, investors and stakeholders. And the same again for the other organization involved.

This activity can, if handled badly, promote heightened levels of uncertainty for your people, increase the flight risk of your brightest talent and create a drop in morale. It will also result in your customers seeking reassurance around continuity of service and quality, and suppliers to ask about certainty of demand and changes to their arrangements. Especially in the post integration phase, you will need to move at pace to minimize this uncertainty and get people out of the other side of that dip as quickly as possible.

As highlighted earlier, it also contains the highest degree of sensitivity and likelihood for the need to keep things confidential. This is in contrast to the default approach we've encouraged throughout around openness and transparency to engender trust and engagement with people. Knowing what you can say, when and why is vital for this element of the plan.

Lastly, it also involves a wider collection of individuals who are less well known to you in terms of managing confidentiality and the other risks associated with your communication and engagement activities. Establishing some shared ground rules and principles that everyone involved can sign up to – buyers, sellers, advisers and other stakeholders – is essential for success.

## Mergers and acquisitions

1. Mergers and acquisitions are at the top of the risk scale.

2. Recognise this lever may not work out; saying no is sometimes the right choice.

3. Tips for navigating this Morphology Map:
   - Be clear on why – it must add value.
   - Know what good looks like when selecting a target – if in doubt, don't do it.
   - Make sure you balance the opportunity against the risk.
   - Appoint the right advisers – and not just those who focus on the money.
   - Consider all aspects of the deal when you get to your go/no-go decision points.
   - Ensure you have a post deal integration plan that maximizes value.
   - Take everyone with you, in the right way, and at the right time.

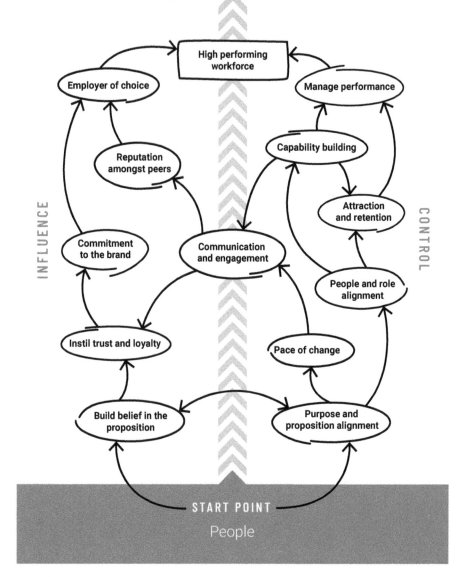

DESIRED OUTCOMES

• Compelling employee proposition    • Goodwill and discretionary effort
• Aligned culture    • Focused retention

High performing workforce

Employer of choice

Manage performance

Reputation amongst peers

Capability building

INFLUENCE

CONTROL

Commitment to the brand

Communication and engagement

Attraction and retention

People and role alignment

Instil trust and loyalty

Pace of change

Build belief in the proposition

Purpose and proposition alignment

START POINT

People

# Chapter 5
# People

*You don't build a business, you build people, the people build the business.*

Zig Ziglar

## Introduction

You might reasonably argue that of all the change levers, this is the most important. As Zig Ziglar implies above, without the right people no business can succeed. In our experience, it is always, always, always about the people. They are the reason why you are able to deliver your products and services. But a high performing workforce gives you so much more:

- motivated staff work together to make the team truly greater than the sum of its parts
- they give discretionary effort willingly (and sometimes unknowingly)
- they are the best advocates for your business – for future employees and customers
- they are solution orientated – always bringing a recommendation, never just a problem
- they provide constructive feedback which supports achieving outcomes
- they create the culture you need to succeed.

Creating an environment that develops and encourages the most able people is far from easy. It takes conscious effort, and specific actions. And, like the culture lever, it is not a one-off project that creates these outcomes. It is an evolution. As your business morphs, your people will need to morph too. After each wave of people change, it will require consistent, persistent effort to maintain the new state you have created, before embarking on the next morph.

# It takes leadership

Creating motivated people starts at the top, which is critical when you choose to pull the people lever. Leaders set direction, but they also set the tone, create the culture and are a significant part of any organization's proposition to potential talent. It is universally true that people follow great leaders, or conversely, in a business context people don't leave organizations, they leave bad bosses. It is the singular responsibility of all leaders to create an environment where people are able to be the best version of themselves. Do this, and results will follow.

As Jim Collins, writing in *Good to Great*,[3] said:

> 'First Who... Then What. We expected that good to great leaders would begin by setting a new vision and strategy. We found instead that they first got the right people on the bus, the wrong people off the bus, and the right people in the right seats – and then they figured out where to drive it.'

Remember that this wasn't something based on a theory of leadership. This is what emerged from one of the most substantial research studies on long-term performance of companies. It turns what we usually think of when we consider strategy on its head. It's much less about a five-year plan and much more about having committed, disciplined people with real integrity on your team who help and support the driver to steer the bus in the right direction. People are more resilient than plans – at least the right people are.

Another thing Jim Collins observed was that organizations which had made the leap from good to great had what he called Level 5 leadership. They are individuals that display a powerful mixture of personal humility and indomitable will. As Collins says:

---

[3] J. Collins, *Good to Great*, First Edition, Random House Business, 4 October, 2001.

'It is very important to grasp that Level 5 leadership is not just about humility and modesty. It is equally about ferocious resolve, an almost stoic determination to do whatever needs to be done to make the company great.'

In our experience, this indomitable will is manifested in the characteristic of drive. The best leaders have an innate sense of drive to get things done – whatever those things might be – but the humility to realize that they don't have all the answers. This drive sets the tone, the ambition and the destination. But they engage with their people in a genuine and meaningful way, using exceptional communication skills and empathy to create trust and belief. They are actively listening and responding to feedback and ideas from their people. And they always deliver on what they say they will. This creates a powerful virtuous cycle as it builds trust and confidence, and creates a highly attractive energy in the team, and organization, for other talented individuals to want to be a part of.

## Purpose and proposition alignment

What you need from your people will be different at different points in your journey as an organization. From start up, to consolidation, to growth, to iteration, to collaboration, formal partnerships or structural changes. Each of these phases require different skills, experience and cultures to succeed.

So, given this, why would you choose to pull this lever, and when? As described in previous chapters there will inevitably be an element of people change as a result of modifying your operating model, the introduction of new products or services, and a merger or acquisition. But in many cases these changes may have a narrow impact on the overall organization and its people, affecting only certain parts of it.

Fundamentally, the people lever can be used irrespective of any structural change activity. You might do this from a defensive position where you start to see your key people metrics in decline. Staff turnover could be increasing, filling vacancies may be becoming harder and take longer, higher levels of sickness and absence might have emerged, or data from staff surveys and exit interviews could be telling you that you have another problem. Responding to all or any of these things with a people change plan is entirely appropriate, but given they are all lagging indicators, they are also telling you that you have had a problem for a while and it will now take more effort to fix it.

The people lever needs to be pulled in rolling waves, aligned to the outcomes that your business is trying to achieve. This means that you need to align your proposition for your people around your purpose and strategy if you are to gravitate to the North Star we talked about in Chapter 2. What type of people, with what skills, experience and motivation do you need to make that North Star your destination? And if you change your purpose or destination through any of the other levers, then you will need to update your people plan too.

Doing this proactively, with intent, and aligned with your other change activities, will get you a positive outcome sooner. But if you find yourself in a situation where the lagging indicators have told you that you have a problem, then you will need to apply a degree of urgency to your people plan.

Building belief in your proposition, aligned to your purpose, is vital if you are to take your people with you. It might not all be in place at the start of your journey but if you can indicate that there is a plan on how to get there it will engender belief. It is your people that drive your competitiveness, your ability to generate a profit or your impact on society, so you cannot afford to get this wrong. And there are real advantages to getting it right as this case study shows.

## Case study: Aligning your proposition around purpose

An independent regulatory body had been administering the payments due to businesses under various policy initiatives for some time. They were asked to take on a similar initiative, but this time for the public. This would mean a significant increase in volumes – tens or even hundreds of thousands of public users compared to the thousands of the businesses they were used to dealing with. This was for a scheme designed to promote early adoption of renewable heating technologies in residential settings.

It would require a new call centre to support the public facing element of the work, which would also be a new operational requirement for the organization.

There was a conscious recognition that this particular purpose required a different approach. Their experience to date had been largely business to business, and their prevailing culture was bureaucratic and risk averse – not ideal for the new venture. They selected a leader who could develop the online solution and build the team and culture that would align to this particular purpose.

The new team was just over 25 people strong in roles spanning audit and assurance functions, through to the call centre operatives, customer service and technical support. In thinking about their proposition, the new leader made a conscious choice to build this team by aligning around their purpose.

Instead of recruiting and inducting new hires on the basis of the technical aspects of their roles alone, they focused on the outcomes they were delivering: the early adoption of renewable technologies, the contribution this would make to the UK's carbon reduction targets, and to the global efforts to tackle climate change.

Adverts were a call to arms to join them in that endeavour. The induction process was also focused on purpose throughout. Sharing the vision for the scheme, the aspiration in terms of performance, the culture they wanted to create, and why that mattered. It even included two days away at an ecology centre. While they were there, they learned all about the factors driving climate change and what both this new scheme and so they, as individuals working on it, were doing to combat it.

The outcome was a manifestation of that well-known story about someone asking a man sweeping the floor at NASA what he was doing and getting the response 'I'm helping put a man on the moon'. People in front-line call centre roles, when asked, said that what they were doing was helping to save the planet.

The impact of aligning their employee proposition around their purpose was borne out in the people metrics. Staff turnover in this division was less than 1 percent compared to 15 percent elsewhere in the organization, and staff engagement hit 74 percent compared to an average of 45 percent elsewhere in the business.

# Pace of change

The pace and complexity of your people change plan will be driven by the scale and scope of the outcomes you are seeking to achieve. Common outcomes we have seen across people change plans is for people to feel motivated, know how they contribute to the success of the organization and are performing well. This is only possible with the following fundamentals in place:

- people being recognized and rewarded for their efforts
- an environment in which people can grow
- support for the development of future leaders
- a fair and understandable performance management regime.

All of these create advocacy for your business as a great place to work. So, a plan that delivers these elements will go a long way, but it does need to work both for the individual and the organization as a whole if it is to be meaningful.

The pace at which you change or modify your people plan will very much depend on your circumstances. But it is important to measure progress and test assumptions regularly. Staff surveys can be an effective tool, and external benchmarking is a powerful mechanism. But there is no substitute for regular, frequent conversations with your people, and triangulating that across the business.

There may be pockets of the business that are struggling with some people related activities more than others. There may be some areas where the proposition is weaker. Consistent feedback and action are fundamental for effective people change. But you need to provide the time and space for people to get on board with the changes you are making – leaving people behind only creates inertia, or worse, a drag factor on the positive progress.

# Attraction and retention

Your people change plan may centre on how you optimize the performance and engagement of your existing staff team – whether that be in developing their capability, retaining key talent or driving performance. But it may also require you to attract and recruit new people – whether that be for new capabilities that you don't have and aren't trainable, or as part of your general growth strategy.

Finding and keeping hold of good people is hard. As with many of the other levers, clarity of purpose and desired outcomes are essential. When thinking about your people this takes the form of creating what has become known as an Employee Value Proposition (EVP). If you prefer to avoid these kinds of labels, just think of this proposition as your internal brand – the way you make yourself attractive to the best and brightest talent, and then keep them for as long as you need them.

There needs to be some natural congruence between your external facing brand and your people proposition, as the alternative would undermine the integrity of both. But whatever your people proposition is, it has a dual purpose. To be compelling enough to attract people into your organization, and then motivate them to a level where they willingly supply discretionary effort – this can be a genuine competitive advantage. Think about the organizations you have worked in where people wanted to go that extra mile and were driven to bring the very best of themselves to their work. How much more effective and impactful were they than those where people clocked in and clocked out, doing the bare minimum required?

There are many pillars to your proposition which are within your control. It is entirely within your gift to put in place all the components that will support your proposition – from the way in which you reward and incentivize your people financially, through to the personal and career development opportunities you provide, and the way you recognize both good and bad performance in the organization. Designing these well not only bring the promises in your proposition to life, they also have the ability to enable (or disable) the culture you want to create.

In seeking to energize and motivate your staff you should first focus on those activities which will create advocacy and belief, as this has the benefit of generating further loyalty and commitment from your existing employees who are the best sales force for finding great people. You can very quickly generate a self-fulfilling and sustainable set of outcomes through a virtuous cycle of brilliant people attracting more brilliant people. We've seen this happen a lot, where influential and successful people who move roles frequently, reconnect with and attract their go-to people. The trick here is doing that on an enduring basis in your core organization.

Whatever the content of the proposition, the employee experience once they arrive must live up to those words. Too often we see externally facing propositions which, when you join the organization, can feel like the emperor's new clothes. People processes and ways of working are misaligned, roles are badly designed and accountability is unclear – all creating a disconnect between the sales pitch and reality. When you are building your plan for the things on the control side of the axes, do so in a way where you are constantly seeking to ensure alignment between words and experience, in order to avoid this outcome.

In an increasingly competitive war for talent, you want to be out in the markets for the people and skillsets you need as soon as possible, but you can only do this credibly if you have done a measure of the thinking on the control side of the Map. Your external facing proposition and your reputation amongst your peers needs to instil belief in prospective candidates that moving to your organization is in their best interests, and will be backed up by reality when they arrive. The level of transparency and openness now provided by websites such as glassdoor.com will soon give you fairly instant feedback on the effectiveness of your external efforts, as well as the internal experience of your people in supporting or undermining your proposition.

## People and role alignment

Ultimately, form follows function and getting your proposition right starts with good quality organization design. Your mission or purpose gives you a definition as to why you exist. Your operating model sets out what you do on a day-to-day basis, sometimes known as service design. Once you know the what, then you can look to the who. How do you best organize that into roles and structures to deliver those services and functions, with the accountabilities and responsibilities in the right place?

**SERVICE DESIGN**

Covers every aspect of how an organization can operate optimally by understanding and re-designing:

· Core service catalogue – the building blocks that make up what you do

· Interfaces and hand-offs needed to make that work (internal and external)

· Policies, procedures and processes that shape the detail and ensure compliance

**ACCOUNTABILITIES AND RESPONSIBILITIES**

**PEOPLE DESIGN**

Covers every aspect of the people capabilities and culture required to bring the service design to life:

· Organization structures

· Role profiles and responsibilities, including interfaces and hand-offs (internal and external)

· Capabilities required to succeed

· Culture required to drive performance

Role clarity is an often underestimated element of a strong employee proposition. Individuals thrive on clarity – knowing what is expected of them and why is a fundamental driver of motivation. It enables people to see what success looks like, know when they have got there, and generates a sense of achievement for having done so, enhancing their motivation – another virtuous cycle.

So, role clarity helps define the capacity you need for the organization to succeed. But in order to ensure you have the right person in the right place doing the right thing you also need to consider the other two c's: capability and culture. We'll look at culture in the next chapter, but capability building is essential to creating high performing teams.

# Capability building

Once you have your organization design you will be able to articulate the capabilities that are needed to succeed in each role. These may be specific technical skills, or specific experience of certain activities. It is the blend of skills and experience that create capabilities that add value to your business. You then have choices about how you create those capabilities. There will be some that need to be bought in and some that you can grow over time by building capability within existing teams. The latter is attractive to internal staff as it provides them with the opportunity to develop new skills and capabilities.

But there will be some elements of your organization design that will demand a level of capability that is already optimized – someone who has been there, seen it, done it and got the t-shirt. These are roles where you cannot take a risk as they are critical to your business succeeding. By and large you will be looking to fill these roles externally, and although there may be limited scope for further development, providing the opportunity to mentor or develop others may well be an attractive part of the proposition for these more experienced hires.

# Case study: A salutary lesson in failing to understand the importance of capability

A medium sized organization employing around 3,500 people had grown steadily and been consistently successful in delivering services to its customers. The regulatory and policy landscape in which the organization operated was due to change considerably in the coming years. In addition to this, there was an increasing demand from their customers to better use technology in the way they provided their services to create a much better – and faster – customer experience.

The Executive team had all the information they needed to recognize that they were facing a twin set of significant changes to their market and the way they needed to provide their services. Given the environment had stayed stable for a relatively long period of time, they lacked the capability to properly understand and influence the changes to the regulatory and policy landscape in which they had to operate. And as they had been providing their services in a largely offline, or paper-based operating model, they also lacked the relevant technology capabilities, from systems to data.

They decided to make some people changes. But not the ones you might expect. Despite these headwinds being on the horizon, they instead chose to focus on making internal efficiency savings, calculating that their longevity and consistent success meant they could afford to shrink their workforce and still deliver their services by reducing their capacity by a third. Their focus was on capacity rather than capability. To compound that error of judgement, the way they decided to make those changes was to offer a voluntary redundancy scheme, rather than being targeted in those areas where change was manageable.

The inevitable happened. Their strongest performers, with the highest levels of capability all put their hands up for voluntary redundancy as they had the confidence of knowing they could secure a role in another organization. This reduced overall capability levels to a point where continuing to provide their existing services to customers was jeopardized. And shortly afterwards, those headwinds hit, and they were completely devoid of the right capabilities in the business to navigate them.

They had undervalued the importance of capability being aligned to the outcomes required for the business to succeed. Not only had they failed to invest in the capabilities required for what was just over the horizon, they had let the wrong people go, finding themselves with critically low levels of capability to be able to respond to the challenges they faced. They went out of existence in less than a year.

# Manage performance

The choice of these words is deliberate. Manage performance. Not performance management. Everyone sees the latter words and sees a HR process, or assumes it is about under performance, or generally gets a sense of dread.

Actively managing performance is a different thing, and it is fundamental to your proposition and the outcomes you want to achieve when you pull the people change lever. The activities on the control side of this Map have taken you through the three simple steps that underpin your ability to manage performance:

1.  Articulate your proposition – be clear on the ask.

2.  Create the right capability – put the support in place to enable people to succeed.

3.  Actively manage performance – hold people to account.

The first step (together with a well-designed role profile and accountabilities) provides clarity, the second provides the tools and support to deliver against that clarity, and they both remove any excuses that prevent you from doing the third. Too often in organizations it is hard to hold people to account as the ask was not clear enough or people can say they haven't been given the tools or support to perform. You must ensure the first two steps are in place if you are to effectively do the third.

If all three steps are in place you can effectively reward and recognize where people are doing well, build on great progress, and offer new opportunities for growth and further capability development. Not only does this generate higher levels of performance from your people, it also has a multiplier effect of delivering higher performance and outcomes across the business, and supports retention and advocacy.

However, there is also a need to recognize and deal with the reality of exiting people who can't reach the required standards of performance. That requirement may seem obvious, but you might also find yourself needing to part company with strong performers as you simply don't need those skills or experience for the next stage of your organization's journey. This is the hardest element of people change and one that leaders and managers struggle with the most. They find it hard to part company with people who have delivered well for them, who they like and rate. But having the wrong set of skills or experience at the wrong time will make it harder for your organization to thrive and may threaten your ability to survive in difficult times if you don't have the right people.

# Case study: The impact on performance of being slow to change the people

An organizational restructure saw a new senior team appointed to run a private sector business, with a good mix of longer serving and newer additions to the team. The external environment had created new competitive pressures which, in turn, had necessitated a shift in purpose and focus to a more dynamic, change-oriented organization, which wasn't the lived experience of large parts of the business.

As the organization embarked on the next phase of its journey, it was clear that there was a distinction between those members of the team who were embracing the new demands, ways of working and competitive pressures, and those who were still operating as they always had done. This was not as simple as those who were new versus existing hires, with some longer serving staff managing to make that adjustment. It was entirely a consequence of the personal leadership qualities being exhibited by each individual.

As time passed, those who were embracing the new ways of working were leaned on by the CEO more often. This manifested itself in broader portfolios, or additional commitments as they garnered a reputation for getting things done. As a consequence, the relative size of the portfolios of other members of the team shrank, and in some cases, poorer performing areas of their responsibilities were moved to the top performing team members.

Initially, those strong performers thrived on this. They welcomed the additional responsibility, the problem solving and change challenges. This created the virtuous cycle of more of the same. But, over a relatively short period of a few months, expressions of resentment and frustration started to be shared. The imbalance of workload and responsibilities across the team was notable. The lack of fairness and equity – in workload and reward – was starting to bite. And, as a consequence, these highly motivated self-starters began to experience a dip in their own morale. The virtuous cycle had become a vicious one.

Within weeks of this being vocalized amongst them, it had a significant impact on team dynamics. The team had split into three cliques, the sense of unity and collective responsibility had been undermined in the process. The strong performers started to push back when asked to take on further areas of responsibility, questioning why they should when their perception was that others weren't pulling their weight.

Within a year, the three strongest performers in this team had left for other roles with competitors. The organization lost their skillsets in a market which had become increasingly competitive, with ever reducing margins. And every one of those individuals took a pay cut in order to get out, so you could say paid a personal financial price too. In the meantime, the poorest performers remained in post and the business they had left behind began to lose market share.

Years later, the CEO of that business would often lament their indecisiveness in taking action around changing out the poorer performing team members. They reflected on the fact that they had clearly known that they weren't making the grade, and this was obvious in the way they had started to move parts of their portfolios to other team members. They often questioned whether that was a conscious choice, or whether it was their way of not wanting to confront the reality, and make hard decisions about people they had known, liked and worked with for many years.

They didn't want to have that conversation where they told them that what had got them to where they were was no longer good enough for the changed environment. But even allowing for that, when the other team members vocalized it, they still chose not to act and, in doing so, sent the organization into a decline, losing competitive advantage and other talented individuals, which several years on they have not yet been able to fully recover from.

# Communication and engagement

Deciding to refresh your people proposition to drive attraction and retention and build a high performing workforce requires almost constant communication and engagement if you are to ensure people are taken on the journey. This can be challenging when the changes being made might feel more subtle to your audience.

- Why does the new proposition differ to what went before?
- How will it feel different for people who work for you?
- What practical things might have changed in terms of tangible rewards or benefits?
- Why should I believe it is worth it?
- How will it benefit me in terms of my career and future with the organization?

These questions and more will all need to be answered if you are to engender the trust and loyalty that you want and need to create the levels of advocacy in your brand and reputation as an employer.

It is also important to avoid the bear trap of speaking to your people as a homogenous group. Some segments of your workforce may be affected more by changes in your proposition when compared to others. At the same time, you want to create a sense of a single purpose and identity within the overarching proposition. Your communication and engagement activities need to be both holistic in nature, as well as segmented and nuanced – acknowledging that the one certain thing you will encounter is people talking to one another, so the clarity of message and relationship between the different component parts is essential.

# Why bother?

We've had lots of conversations over our careers with leaders in organizations who struggle with the people change lever. It's hard work. It takes time. And it involves people, who can be unpredictable and challenging at times. But it is the lever that can have the biggest single impact on the performance of your business.

The best people plans deliver game-changing outcomes.

- Staff teams are consistently aligned around the purpose and objectives of the organization, creating an accelerant to achieving them.

- Absolute clarity on individual accountability and the freedom people have to operate in, enables swift decision making and progress.

- Reward is fair and great performance is recognized, creating a multiplier effect in terms of motivation and loyalty.

- Poor performers are actively managed, and sometimes leave the organization, instilling a stronger sense of fairness, equity and drive.

All of these outcomes have words which describe momentum in them. Your people are the biggest determinants of pace and progress – getting this right means getting to your goals faster. It really is a classic case of outputs being greater than the sum of its parts.

## Don't forget your culture

It is almost impossible to pursue the development of a plan for the people change lever without also addressing elements of the Culture Morphology Map. People will not only be the single biggest determinant of your success, but also your culture. You need the right capability to lead and drive the culture, with not only leaders, but everyone embodying it in everything they do.

## BITE SIZE MORPHOLOGY
## People

1. Without the right people no business can succeed.

2. The quality of leadership and management is vital to success.

3. Tips for navigating this Morphology Map:

   · Your purpose and people proposition must align – it builds trust and loyalty.

   · People change needs to be at a pace that allows people to get on board.

   · Your organizational design needs to support both your purpose and people proposition.

   · If you don't have the right capabilities, go and find them.

   · Look after your existing people – develop their capability where you can.

   · Manage performance – if you can't change the people, change the people.

   · Communicate thoughtfully and continuously – know your audiences.

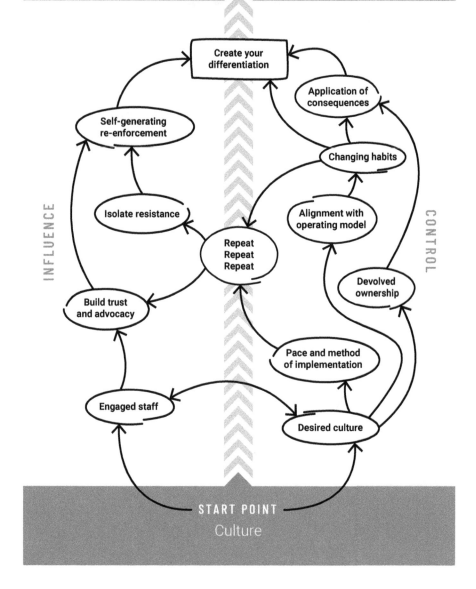

DESIRED OUTCOMES
· Cultural alignment    · Multiplier effect on performance
· Shared purpose        · Consistent employee experience

Create your differentiation

Application of consequences

Self-generating re-enforcement

Changing habits

INFLUENCE

CONTROL

Isolate resistance

Alignment with operating model

Repeat Repeat Repeat

Devolved ownership

Build trust and advocacy

Pace and method of implementation

Engaged staff

Desired culture

START POINT
Culture

# Chapter 6
# Culture

*Culture is a set of living relationships working towards a shared goal. It's not something you are, it's something you do.*

D. Coyle[4]

## Introduction

The culture of an organization is its glue, its DNA. It fills the gaps between the processes and work instructions and binds staff together with a common purpose. Get it right and it will make your organization sing.

We hear people claim that measuring culture isn't possible. It is, and it is an essential barometer for organizational health. There are a wealth of data points available to you from existing processes: staff surveys, exit interviews or 360 feedback tools. But they need to be consciously and continuously used in a way that enables trends to be analysed over time.

Organizations who recognize the competitive advantage that culture brings them also design this into the way they manage the performance of their people, focusing on the cultural dimensions as well as task performance. All of these methods provide you with data points that can evidence how engaged and invested your people are in your culture: do they live and breathe it day in and day out or just pay lip service? As Daniel Coyle says: 'It's not something you are, its something you do'. And of course, the most obvious metric for the return on investment in the culture you create, is the improvement in all of your business performance metrics, right through to the bottom line.

---

[4] D. Coyle, *The Culture Code*, First Edition, Random House Business, 1 February, 2018.

However you choose to assess and measure your culture, companies that create compelling cultures have a number of common features:

- strong alignment between the company's purpose, strategies and business goals and the cultural features required to enable success

- leadership that continuously role model the culture required

- coherent and regular communication that speaks to all employees and reinforces the culture

- staff that are cared for, listened to, nurtured and feel part of the organization

- a healthy and vibrant social network that underpins the work environment.

The net effect of getting your culture right is a high performing team that goes the extra mile, where staff feel a strong sense of loyalty and belonging. It also differentiates you from your competition, both in the market and in terms of attracting and retaining staff. In a study by Glassdoor, 77 percent of 5,000 respondents said they would consider a company's culture before applying for a job. Over half said it was more important than salary when it came to job satisfaction.[5]

Unfortunately, we have all experienced at one time or another organizations where the culture is poor, or even toxic. It can breed a real sense of fear among staff who are disengaged and have little or no loyalty to the company or each other. Not surprisingly this manifests itself in poor business results, high staff turnover and a bad reputation.

So, getting your culture to be enhancing and not destructive is vitally important. But it's not a one-off intervention. Like the people lever, enhancing your culture is something that you morph through in rolling waves. Each leg of your cultural journey needs to be driven in a programmatic way which is consistent and coherent if it is to take effect. Put another way, it is not a one-off project. As one organization's cultural blueprint once said: this is not a project, it is a way of being.

---

[5] Glassdoor's Mission & Culture Survey (2019), www.glassdoor.co.uk

Your cultural development plan needs to constantly reinforce, revisit and evolve – morphing with your business.

# Define your desired culture

As with all of the change levers, your purpose gives you your North Star. Why you exist and what you are trying to achieve defines the kind of culture you need. A start up in a groundbreaking new area will need agility, innovation and the willingness to try and fail fast to gain competitive advantage. A mature business in a longstanding and regulated industry sector with limited opportunities for innovation will need to continuously find ways to differentiate their offer from their competitors, whilst always delivering in a way which is efficient and compliant.

So, the basic building blocks for the creation, development and evolution of your culture are your purpose, strategies and business goals. These provide the framework in which your employees operate and the North Star for the required culture to deliver against them. Your culture should define what is encouraged, discouraged, accepted or rejected, and each of these need to be communicated, demonstrated and continually reinforced.

Defining your desired culture should never be done in isolation. Co-creating it with your people means they will share a sense of ownership with the outcome and understand why it matters, as does their part in bringing it to life. And there will be people who are naturally already role models for your desired culture, so can quickly lead by example. This provides a strong foundation for what you want the whole organization to look and feel like.

# Implementing change

However you choose to describe the culture you want to see – values statements, charters, behavioural frameworks, blueprints – it has to be done in a way and at a pace which is relevant to your business and your people at that point in time. And of course, you should involve your people in co-creating this in order to build advocacy and overcome resistance.

So, what are some of the common mistakes that organizations make when they try to modify culture?

- Give to it HR, because they know about people. Yes, the HR team are the function that owns the people policies and processes, but they alone do not set the culture. Culture is role modelled by everyone in a leadership or management position in the organization.

- Spend lots of time wordsmithing values. Corporate values are important but they must have meaning to your staff. Generic values that proclaim the business is professional, customer focused and inclusive are just that, generic; they do not convey what is important to your business and what differentiates you from others.

- Focus on behaviours in isolation. As one of the most often used definitions of culture goes – it is the thing that people do when no-one else is looking. You want people to behave in a way that is aligned with your cultural aspirations in everything they do. But a focus purely on behaviours in isolation of the processes and ways of working within the organization will achieve very little.

- Put posters on a wall and expect everyone to suddenly change how they work. And, as one of the best proponents of cultural change that we have ever worked with says to senior teams at the end of design sessions: 'What you'll notice here is at no point has anyone mentioned posters'. For sure, collateral that reinforces your message in whatever way is helpful as a communication tool, but sticking posters on the walls with your values or behaviours on it won't miraculously change your culture on its own.

Fundamentally, enhancing your culture is a capability development activity. You need to be able to articulate what you want to see (your cultural blueprint), put in place the support to enable people to do that (capability building) and then apply consequences for adherence or non-adherence (manage performance). The bottom line is improving the culture of an organization is a team game – everyone is involved and everyone needs to take part if you are to create the culture you need to drive business performance.

# Case study: Getting culture change wrong

A large UK organization operating out of a number of sites embarked on a programme of culture change. The drivers for this decision were varied and included high staff turnover, low levels of engagement evidenced through the annual staff survey, and competitors in the same industry creating more compelling employee propositions based on their culture and working environment. Over two thirds of the organization were call centre operations with traditionally low paid, process driven teams.

The HR team were asked to lead the work and proceeded to set up a series of focus groups around the country to hear what people valued about the current culture and what they thought should change. These were listening exercises which created an opportunity to vent for employees and almost every session managed to create a negative cycle of energy and complaints. Very few of them even got close to defining what good would look like.

In the absence of those future facing data points, the HR team analysed the feedback by creating word clouds which highlighted the strength of feeing around the most negative features. The most notable words were slow, bureaucratic and disempowering, with a strong theme about a lack of recognition for good performance.

The HR team recommended a new set of value statements which would be the opposite of this. They proposed:

- we work at pace to deliver for our customers
- we eliminate bureaucracy wherever we see it
- we empower our people to make the right choices.

These were agreed by the senior team as being just what the organization needed and were rolled out with a big internal fanfare. Videos, written communication and team leader briefing packs. Branded merchandise including credit card size reminders of these three statements for every employee, mouse mats on desks with them printed on it, new screensavers and posters in every staff area and kitchen.

All call centre team leaders were briefed that they now had the autonomy to deal with a range of customer issues which had formerly required escalation. This was done in order to drive the empowerment they were aspiring to in the value statement, and with the hope that it would also create higher levels of ownership to tackle issues of bureaucracy locally.

It took a matter of days for this to fall apart. The minute a team leader tried to exercise this newfound autonomy, they bumped up against a process or a system approval requirement which prevented them from taking action. The net result was that the culture change programme had the entirely opposite effect than had been hoped for – morale plummeted further on the back of being given hope that something would change, only to be disappointed, and staff turnover continued to rise.

They had failed to create any ownership amongst their people for the culture they wanted to see. They hadn't aligned it around their purpose and strategy. And they had only tackled behaviours rather than the infrastructure required to bring it to life. The poor implementation of this also deepened cynicism within the organization, so when they tried to address the failure with a new programme that had learned lessons from this one, their starting point was a level of deeply ingrained negativity, increasing resistance and delaying the ability to deliver outcomes.

## Devolved ownership

Bringing your desired culture to life starts at the top, as that sets the tone. The behaviours and actions displayed by those in leadership positions are vitally important. If you don't believe this, try a version of this experiment which we used with a leadership team who doubted the significance of the impact of their own behaviour on others.

We asked the CEO of a relatively small organization, employing around 150 people, who sat in an open plan office, to always have a copy of a particular publication on the corner of their desk. And to carry it with them in and out of meetings. This made it visible to everyone whether they approached them at their desk or engaged with them in a meeting setting. Within less than a month we counted 40 people who had started subscribing to the same publication, demonstrating to the CEO the hidden power of their behaviour on the choices made by employees. It made them realise why what they did every day as the leadership team was integral to realizing the cultural ambitions of the organization.

But even if you have the most culturally aligned leadership team, if any of the middle managers are off key, then they can de-rail your cultural ambitions quicker than you might imagine. The wheels come off because the parts of the organization that are adopting the new ways of working to create the required culture notice that they are, and others aren't.

Worse still, there is no consequence for that. This very quickly turns your early adopters and advocates into people who opt out and the virtuous cycle you are seeking to establish turns into a vicious one, and momentum is lost. This requires you to ensure that everyone understands their personal accountability for demonstrably living the culture you want in your organization. It needs the active application of consequences – rewarding those who do, and managing those who don't.

# Operating model alignment

Culture isn't just about behaviours. It is enabled (or disabled) by ways of working. Your operating model is vital to bringing your culture to life. As the previous case study illustrated, if one of your cultural principles is to ensure that there is autonomy so that people closest to the issues have the ability to make decisions, but your operating model contains policies or processes which require constant upward permission for signing things off, then your operating model is disabling your culture.

The elements required for improving your culture need to be embedded into your operating model and your people proposition. How you manage performance needs to reinforce the importance of the cultural characteristics you need to succeed. How you design your operating model needs to enable rather than disable the culture. It provides you with a competitive advantage over other organizations. As we said in the opening chapter, if two businesses have the same infrastructure and resources at their disposal, the culture within their organizations is the differentiator. *What* you do matters, but *how* you do it creates a performance advantage between you and your competitors.

In today's world, the other dynamic that needs to be considered from an operating model perspective is the arrangements you have in place for remote or hybrid working. This can enable or inhibit the culture you want to create – whether with new or existing teams. Whilst the COVID-19 pandemic saw all kinds of creative online solutions, which are all good things to have in your toolkit, the simple truth is that the biggest accelerant for creating a strong team or cultural identity is face-to-face interaction. As Margaret Heffernan says, 'social capital is created from the conversations outside of set piece meetings or events'.[6]

In one organization we worked with, the pandemic had created an opportunity to recruit from a wider geography than just near their HQ location. Teams quickly formed that spanned all parts of the UK and, in one case, even Europe. They were conscious that whilst this provided an upside in terms of accessing higher levels of capability rather then being geographically constrained, they were going to have to take conscious steps to create a team identity and culture. They did this by supporting the maximum amount of flexibility and work–life balance that was possible, with one ask in return: that everyone came together at a set frequency for a full team day, including an overnight and social event. This provided the building blocks for creating social capital amongst the team members, as well as opportunities to collaborate, learn and grow together.

This was then reinforced in the intervening period by short stand-up meetings twice a week where those connections – and importantly, the humour and personal familiarity that are the hallmarks of social capital – could be maintained remotely. Indeed, when those meetings were withdrawn as the team grew, the gap created by the lack of connection and coherence was quickly evident. The leader of that team had underestimated how those touchpoints were essential to team identity and being able to maintain the culture that had been created.

# Changing habits

Peter Drucker is often misattributed with the quote: 'Culture eats strategy for breakfast'. What he actually said is: 'Culture, no matter how

---

[6]  M. Heffernan, *Forget the Pecking Order at Work*, www.ted.com/talks/margaret_heffernan_forget_the_pecking_order_at_work

defined, is singularly persistent.'[7] There is no doubt that this makes it hard to modify or influence. But fundamentally, this helps or hinders your ability to do everything else that we have written about in this book. When you build your plan, understand that it is a long haul, but worth it. It requires central, co-ordinated drive for longer than you would expect – even when you have high degrees of local accountability.

Ensure that you allow for sufficient capacity and capability to support a relentless programme of reinforcement over months and years. This will make sure you can create a bow wave to overcome the inevitable resistance you will encounter – the faster you reach that tipping point, the faster you can start to generate the momentum from the snowball effect.

This momentum is only possible by breaking old habits and creating new ones. New hires will find it easier to adopt new habits if those expectations are clearly set out through their recruitment and onboarding. The ask for existing employees is harder as you need them to first unlearn their current habits and replace them with new ones. The easiest way to do this is to ask people to make small, incremental changes, encouraging and rewarding them along the way. One of the best books on this is James Clear's *Atomic Habits*[8] which unpacks a lot of the psychology – and tips – on how to make new habits stick.

One of the most effective ways to extend advocacy around the value of new habits and drive cultural change is through peer-to-peer interventions. Examples from managers or teams on how adopting the ways of working have helped them achieve outcomes creates a sense of energy and, on an unconscious level, a degree of competitiveness to drive action. And the most important habit of all to build into your culture – whatever features or qualities it has – is one of feedback. Effective feedback loops across all levels of the organization – not limited to line manager interactions –

---

[7] P. Drucker, *Culture, No Matter How Defined, is Singularly Persistent*, www.drucker.institute

[8] J. Clear, *Atomic Habits*, First edition, Random House Business, 18 October, 2018.

is a powerful accelerant for embedding new habits. Start with a feedback habit, and the others will follow.

## There must be consequences

Whilst most people will focus on reinforcing feedback, there does need to be the application of consequences too. Without the application of consequences, your cultural ambitions are toothless. Setting out in the right direction and implementing a coherent and well communicated plan will get you off to a great start. There will be early adopters or advocates within your workforce who will both buy into it and have a natural propensity to operate in the way you want them to. But without the application of consequences, you will never bring all the people to the place you need.

However you manage performance, alignment and role modelling of the organization's culture needs to be rewarded and incentivized, and action taken where it is not evident. If you can't change the people, then you need to change the people. And as we described in the previous chapter, that might mean changing out people who have delivered well for you in the past, but now you need a different culture that they can't deliver on.

Cultural improvements will only ever be sustained through a clearly defined, driven and enduring programme of activities to support your outcomes, complemented by the fearless and consistent application of consequences for non-adherence. Until you get to a point where it is naturally self-generating and sustainable.

## Case study: You only need one metaphoric head on a spike to show you mean business

A large teaching hospital within the NHS was embarking on an ambitious cultural change programme. Many reports and reviews had highlighted a number of challenges with aspects of their culture, including regulatory inspections. They knew that one of their biggest challenges would be in tackling the unacceptable behaviour of some highly capable and skilled clinicians.

They approached the work in the right way. They resourced it with the right capability and capacity to achieve their outcomes. They engaged with every segment of their workforce in a meaningful way. They actively listened to ensure that the root cause analysis around the behavioural and infrastructural challenges were triangulated. And they ensured there was ownership and input from all staff groups on the shape of the culture they wanted to create.

They needed to ensure that every part of the organization understood that what they did was no longer good enough. *How* they worked was as, if not more, important. They decided that they would start to review people's performance on both their technical competence and the way they behaved.

They gathered a few hundred of the most senior leaders of the organization together. These spanned doctors, nurses, managers and support partners. The CEO unveiled the new cultural aspirations and the next phases of the programme of work. And they were crystal clear with everyone in the room that they, as the leaders of the organization, were expected to not only help drive this forward but be exemplars of the new culture.

Someone asked the question: 'But what happens if someone who is great at their job continues to behave badly?' The CEO calmly provided the following response: 'We'll say thank you for your service, and goodbye.' You could hear the murmurs of surprise ripple round the room. The next question was asked: 'Yes, but what happens if someone who is the most eminent, world-renowned expert in their field behaves badly?'

And without missing a beat, the CEO equally as calmly said: 'We'll say thank you for your service, and goodbye.'

As the room emptied you got a palpable sense of hope that he meant it, but disbelief that it would ever happen. But two weeks later it did. Someone who was absolutely at the peak of their technical competence, but had a history of behaving badly with their colleagues, was removed from their post. This was the CEO's metaphoric head on a spike. It showed he was serious.

It gave a significant morale lift to those segments of the workforce that had traditionally been on the receiving end of the bad behaviour, and it sent the clearest possible signal to others who might have doubted his intent that he was serious. He only had to do it once. And the trick was he did it early, acted swiftly and was clear about why. It provided the equivalent of a rocket boost to their cultural change ambitions.

## Repeat, repeat, repeat: aspire for self-generation

The aspiration of any culture change activity should be that it reaches a point where it becomes self-generating through the reinforcement that happens every day in the way that people role model the desired culture. But it takes time and lots of repetition to get to this point. So, when you build your culture plan, the support for staff – in whatever form that takes – should be repeated and often. It should apply to existing staff, but also be an integral part of the induction of any new employees. As soon as they arrive in the organization they should understand what is expected so that they begin their journey in a way which is aligned around the culture required. Those expectations should be clear from the start, and the support should be provided to enable them to do that the minute they join.

The repeated support interventions should create a never-ending drumbeat or mantra. Almost to the point where you think you are saying it too often. If you get this right, soon you will hear the words being quoted back at you, then quoted back at you consistently, then embedded into the language used when people describe working there. And finally, it simply becomes just the way we do things round here. This is the same model as any development activity where you move through unconscious incompetence (I didn't think about culture) to conscious incompetence (I can see what is required of me now, but I have no idea how to do it), through to conscious competence.

This takes time to develop, which is why it needs repetition. It is not a one off technical skill, rather a highly nuanced mix of how to show up (behaviour) and how challenge ways of working so that they support rather than block the culture you want to see (infrastructure). And while it is driven by activities on the control side of the Map, it also underpins your influence activities, as it will isolate resistance and help you build the trust and advocacy you need to reach the self-generation stage.

# Make your culture your differentiator

By now, we hope you can see that culture not only matters, but it is absolutely critical to success. When you get it right, aligned around your purpose and outcomes, it gives you a competitive advantage. It should be a fundamental design principle for your operating model. It supports the people required to take new products or services to market. It is essential for making mergers and acquisitions deliver their hoped for value. And it is fundamental to explaining why, and when you pull the people lever. Every one of these things are in service of driving performance. If you are losing margin or market share and heading towards a position of distress, you might be driven to any of the other levers. But modifying and improving your culture could, in itself, be enough to move you from survival mode to thriving.

You also have the opportunity to create a further accelerant through a virtuous cycle. All of us have our own styles and preferences and will thrive in some cultures better than others. Choosing an organization where there is a more natural fit for your own cultural preferences will enhance your motivation and output. Delivering your cultural improvement plan will create advocates for your culture who will, in turn, attract other like-minded individuals, further embedding your cultural aspirations.

## Case study: How hiring on cultural fit drives performance

One of the advantages of working in transformation or change programmes is the ability to create a time limited team. You are generally looking for high levels of experience and capability, as these project teams tend to be the catalysts for the change you want to see, the experts in guiding an organization on how to achieve their outcomes, and role models for the culture you want to create.

As with any recruitment process, once you get to your shortlist, you have a list of people who are technically able to do the job. So that's not what gets them hired. You often hear people talk about fit. What that really means is their fit with the current culture or, often in programme teams, the culture the organization is trying to create. These additional resources add a cost burden to the business, so you need them to deliver value quickly. They need to get through the storming, norming and forming phases and create a tight knit, purposeful team as quickly as possible.

Recognising this, we tried experimenting when putting our programme teams together. Instead of hiring on technical skill, we hired on cultural fit. The culture needed for the programme team *and* the organization they were working in. The leader of that team – regardless of where the role sat in the structure – would interview everyone first. The purpose of this was to assess cultural fit. Using three simple questions they were able to quickly ascertain their fit for the team, whether they were likely to succeed in the organization, and that they had the necessary level of drive to deliver outcomes at pace, which was essential.

They simply opened with: Tell me your potted history? (and listened actively to how people chose to answer that question); and then asked: What is it that makes you punch the air with the joy when you feel like you had a great day?; What makes you feel like the opposite, going home and feeling dejected?; and finally: What is the biggest risk you've ever taken? The answers to these core questions provided enough insight as to whether they could operate in the way that was required, in that environment.

Only once they passed that cultural fit test, did they get to a second stage with the colleagues they would be working with on a day-to-day basis. That final interview was a further validation from them around cultural fit, but also gave them a chance to test the technical competence and approaches they brought. This way of hiring ensured the commonality across all of the team was cultural alignment. And it makes us wonder whymore organizations don't take this approach to all of their recruitment.

At one organization where we did this, there was a major drive on diversity and attracting a broader range of experiences (as well as protected characteristics) into the business. The lead for this work was reflecting on how the transformation team was a conundrum. He said:

> 'On the one hand your team are incredibly similar and it made me think you lacked diversity; but the more I've thought about it, the more I've realised that the similarity is about their attitude and approach. When you look at them as individuals I can see that you have probably the most diverse team in the organization – different ages, life experiences, education and professional training.'

And there's your added bonus. Hiring on cultural fit transcends all those other biases and perceptions in traditional recruitment processes and creates more diverse teams.

## BITE SIZE MORPHOLOGY
### Culture

1. The culture of your organization is its glue – it makes it greater than the sum of its parts.

2. Getting this right is a differentiator – driving performance and competitive advantage.

3. Tips for navigating this Morphology Map:
   - Define the culture you need to deliver your purpose – engage your people in the process.
   - Changing culture needs everyone to take part – devolve ownership.
   - Make sure your operating model supports the culture you aspire to.
   - Asking people to break old habits and create new ones takes time – be patient.
   - Ensure there are consequences – both for role modelling and resisting.
   - Changing culture is a long game – repeat, repeat, repeat until it becomes self-generating.

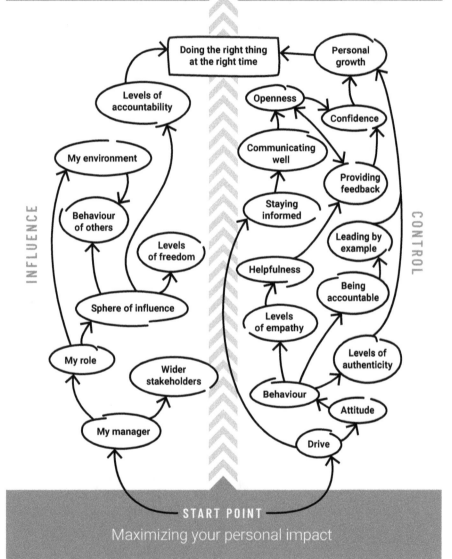

DESIRED OUTCOMES
• Improved performance    • Maximized personal impact
• Motivation              • Self satisfaction

Doing the right thing at the right time

Personal growth

Levels of accountability

Openness

Confidence

My environment

Communicating well

Providing feedback

Behaviour of others

Staying informed

Leading by example

Levels of freedom

Helpfulness

Being accountable

Sphere of influence

Levels of empathy

Levels of authenticity

My role

Wider stakeholders

Behaviour

Attitude

My manager

Drive

INFLUENCE

CONTROL

START POINT
Maximizing your personal impact

# Chapter 7
# Maximizing your personal impact

*How do you become better tomorrow? By improving yourself, the world is made better. Be afraid of standing still. Forget your mistakes but remember what they taught. So how do you become better tomorrow? By becoming better today.*

Benjamin Franklin

## Introduction

You could argue the only reason people go to work is to earn money. However, for many, money is only one of several motivating factors, and in almost every survey of individuals we've seen, it is never the number one reason. People are driven by a wide range of motivations, including:

- a sense of purpose
- being able to make a difference
- being able to learn and grow as individuals
- doing interesting/challenging work
- earning respect
- achieving social recognition and affirmation
- enjoying the structure of work and how that supports mental well-being.

Whatever your motivation, it is vitally important to ensure that you feel valued and you can see that you are making a contribution to the organization you work for. Of course, this is not always true – how often have we come into contact with someone who says they hate their job? The simple truth is it doesn't have to be that way but to avoid this trap, it does require you to take ownership of your career and working life.

The world of work today is complicated, particularly with the increase in roles that can be done from home. It can also be very stressful, especially when the organization you work for is going through a time of change. Navigating your way through all this is not easy.

In recognition of this, the Morphology Map for this chapter has more complexity. But it is most probably the richest in terms of helping you to consider the things you can directly address and control and to think about those aspects of your working environment that you need to start to try and influence. The sum of this will then enable you to build a plan so that you can start to take ownership of your own performance and contribution.

# Show up for work

People who are successful at work come in all shapes and sizes. Extroverts and introverts. Activists and reflectors. And every other dimension you can imagine. The commonality across them all is how they choose to show up. They display and demonstrate a drive to contribute and succeed, day in, day out. Of course, none of us are superheroes – we all have good days and bad days – but the most effective individuals show up consistently in a way that makes a positive difference more days than they don't.

As Franklin's quote at the start of this chapter asserts, as well as showing up in a way which is positive and constructive, every high performer has a number of other strong characteristics. They usually operate with humility and are endlessly curious about how they, and the organizations they work for, can improve. Actively listening to those around them so they can take decisions which are balanced and greater than just their singular focus. And proactively seeking feedback on how to improve, role modelling this by being a generous provider of feedback to others too.

This humility and quest for feedback is an important foundation for the influence side of this Morphology Map. Whatever your personal goals are, you will need help to achieve them. That means building an open and honest rapport with your manager and other stakeholders within your sphere of influence. And you can engage with them on this journey by first seeking feedback. Doing so will see you demonstrate your humility, your willingness to learn in the pursuit of your aspirations and will support your own personal growth and impact.

## Take ownership

One of the key outcomes of this active management of your own performance is to align your activity with your motivation. Too often we see people in roles they stumbled into without a clear plan. Or jobs that they feel trapped in because of wider personal commitments making it feel like change is too risky. But the world of work is so wide and varied that there is a place for everyone in an organization where they feel they belong, doing the thing that they are best at. This is the personal equivalent of the purpose we've spoken about for the other change levers.

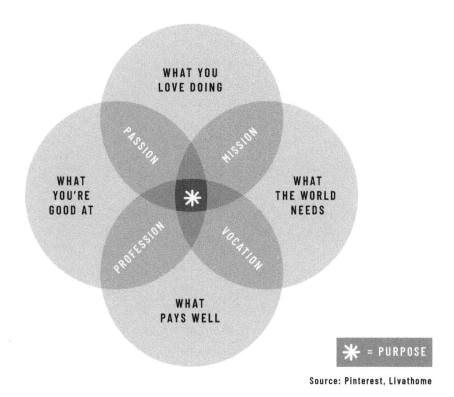

Source: Pinterest, Livathome

Yet despite this, too few people start by aligning their own motivation and preferences with the work that they do. Sure, there may be some of you reading this thinking, well I always wanted to be an astronaut but that's not going to happen. But, of course, we're not talking about pipe dreams or fantasy jobs. What we're saying is, if you have a grounded and conscious understanding of what motivates you at work and the kinds of organizations where you might feel at home, it will provide you with a solid foundation for achieving your career aspirations.

So, once you have grounded your *why* (motivation) and your *where* (organizations) you can build a plan based on the *what* and the *how*. What do you need to do to make this a reality and how will you go about it?

## Empower yourself

This Morphology Map should assist you in developing a plan that will enable you to support your personal growth. The plan should be about how you maximize your impact, but in service of your own aspirations rather than someone else's. When those two align, you will create a virtuous cycle and multiplier effect. This alignment will also be evident in the authenticity of the narrative and stories you tell during your influencing activities.

Your plan will, like the plans you create for the other levers in this book, need to iterate over time, responding to learning and feedback. There will be many routes for you to get to your desired destination. This will allow you to increase your chances of doing the right thing at the right time, for yourself and the organization you work for. As John Maxwell, the author and speaker, once said: 'Successful people and unsuccessful people do not vary greatly in their attributes. They vary in their desire to reach their potential.'

## Understand yourself and others

Of course, none of this is as straightforward as it seems, primarily because there are people involved, all of whom have different characteristics and motivation. Listening to and understanding them is critical if you are to be able to operate cohesively and constructively. At the same time, you need to understand yourself. It needs a level of self-awareness which takes time to develop in a way which is authentic and triangulated.

Remember, we are notoriously poor judges of our own impact on others – under valuing the positive attributes and impact we bring to individuals and teams, whilst also having blind spots as to the things that we might be able to do differently to enhance our impact.

# Case study: Understanding yourself and others

There are numerous tools and techniques that can be used to understand the core characteristics of individuals: Myers Briggs, Insights, Hogan, OPQ, Fibro... the list is endless. They can be a helpful way to stimulate your own self-awareness, deepening your understanding of why you react in certain ways in particular situations, and help you understand your relative strengths and weaknesses. But perhaps more powerfully, if you understand the core characteristics of yourself you can also increase your awareness of these qualities in others, allowing you to improve the effectiveness of your working relationships with them.

The benefits of this approach played out in a large multi-national organization that was seeking to enhance the skills and understanding of their top 100 employees. As part of this, a subset of the top 100 undertook a role-playing exercise that was designed to help individuals understand which of four broad characteristic groups they belonged to: Sovereign, Warrior, Nurturer and Dreamer.

Not unsurprisingly, given it was the top 100 employees, many of those taking part were characterized as Warriors. This archetype was defined as the go-getters, the big hitters, the action orientated. Interestingly the most senior individual in the room wasn't. His underlying characteristic type was that of a Nurturer. The positive traits of this archetype were a good listener, emotionally intelligent and supportive. However, the negative traits were: suffocating, intrusive and unfocused. These negative traits were in direct conflict with the Warriors in the room.

This insight was pivotal in changing the way in which others then engaged with this senior individual. In particular, one relationship, which had been fractious and confrontational, became far more constructive and cohesive. The change was not driven by the more senior individual, but rather by the more junior individual who, by recognizing his own strengths and weaknesses, adjusted his behaviour to better align and work with his boss. As a result of this, they both enjoyed a far more positive working relationship built on trust and openness.

# Make a plan

What would a good plan to maximize your own personal impact look like? Each plan will be personal to you and the situation in which you find yourself. However, there are a number of building blocks that you can use to help you construct your plan.

- Use the data from your most recent performance management review or appraisal. This will provide you with an objective view of the things that you are doing well and the areas where you need to develop based on what you are currently doing – the perfect start point to go from good to great.

- If you want to progress further than your current role – either to a more senior role in your current discipline or move to something new – seek further insight into what you need to do to make that a reality. What different skills do you require? What further knowledge do you need? What personal attributes should you develop? What elements of your personality do you need to bring to the fore?

- Seek feedback. The only way to improve your self-awareness and understanding of your personal impact is to ask for feedback – another thing that we are notoriously bad at doing. Consider what it is you want to understand and ask those questions specifically. For example, I'm looking to improve my personal impact so I am actively seeking feedback on how others experience me; or, I would appreciate your honest assessment of where I do well and less well at x, y or z.

- Observe and copy. There will be people that you admire in your organization, based on the way they do their job and conduct themselves. These role models will display attributes that you can observe and copy. This helps you build those attributes that you believe will maximize your own impact into your own persona. This can range from simple things like how to organize and run a meeting, through to ways to cope with a high pressure or challenging work situation. Even better, reach out to these role models and ask them for feedback or their support as a mentor. Everyone worries about asking these kinds of questions, but people are generally grateful to be asked, and are always happy to help.

- Check and iterate. Changing behaviours and learning new ways of doing things takes time to become a new habit which you can do without deliberate focus. A simple way to ensure you are making progress is to create the space to reflect on a regular basis. If you've asked for feedback from people, let them know the new thing you are practising and ask them how they think you are doing. Journaling can be a useful tool and there are many products available which will help put structure around the capturing of goals, reflections, progress and next steps. Constantly reflecting and course correcting will help you embed the new habits and ways of working you want to create.

- Make time for yourself. It's all too easy to be swept along with the pace of work, to the extent that you really don't have any time to take stock. Although this can feel exhilarating, it doesn't create sufficient space and balance between thinking and doing. Done to excess it can also be highly stressful and have a detrimental impact on your mental and physical health. It is important that you create the opportunity to pause and take stock with some simple reflective questions such as: Can I do this task in a better, faster or cheaper way? What would make the task or activity easier? I tried something new today, how did it go? Looking ahead, what are the things that I can prioritize which will really make the difference to reaching my goals? The trick here is to ensure you have the time and space to consider the work you are doing and how to do it smarter.

# Know when it is time to move on

Sometimes, maximizing our personal impact is best delivered by making a change. This can be challenging to confront, especially if you enjoy your role and where you work. But as we've said elsewhere in the book, organizations go through different stages, and they need different capabilities and experiences to deliver those requirements. Being aware of what the organization needs from you, and whether you can meet those expectations, is fundamental to you retaining control of that choice and maximizing your impact.

## Case study: Changing your leader to change the outcome

A number of years ago a medium-sized organization completed a management buy-out (MBO) from a major multi-national. The buy-out was stimulated by the multi-national realizing that the entity in question didn't really fit as part of its long-term strategy. As a consequence, it lacked direction and its performance was suffering through neglect.

The options were stark: close and make everyone redundant, or offer the opportunity for an MBO to the existing management team. The MBO option was chosen and was led by someone who was highly experienced in change and ideally suited to the rigours of negotiating a complex MBO in the face of the legal might of the multi-national. There was a clarity and unity of purpose in the MBO team as a result of the leadership being provided, and after several months the exit was achieved.

Even more importantly there was a plan on what to do next. This was wide-ranging, encompassing both structural and people changes, through to new IT investment and implementation. The impact on staff was significant, as they all saw the benefits of the changes being made, and after a long period of drifting there began to be a real sense of momentum and hope.

As a consequence, the organization began to turn a corner. The leader of the MBO team became the CEO and the organization became more efficient, dynamic, profitable and started to grow. Within a few years the ship was stable and sustainable and the management team below the Board – having been given room to take up their new challenges – were growing the business and themselves.

As time went on it became more and more evident that the CEO who had been the driving force during a period of significant change, was now becoming more and more distant from the day-to-day activity of the business and, more importantly, employees. This distancing was further emphasized by fractures that appeared in the Board around future strategy discussions, where the CEO was pushing for further aggressive growth through a merger or acquisition based on his personal experience and skillsets. The leadership qualities that had been necessary to get the organization to this point, weren't necessarily what was needed for the next stage of the journey.

Inevitably these tensions resulted in the Board coming to the decision that a change of CEO was required. Understandably this was a painful and bruising experience on a personal level, but they needed a new leader who could take the shareholders and staff on a new journey. This was less about large-scale change and was centred on ensuring that the organization focused on delighting its customers and growing its reputation – the consequence of which would be improvements to both its top-line and bottom-line performance. The result? With the right skills for the next stage of the journey in place, the organization began to achieve outstanding financial results and significant value to its shareholders.

**BITE SIZE MORPHOLOGY**

Maximizing your personal impact

1. Take ownership of your career.

2. Be clear about your motivation and purpose.

3. Tips for navigating this Morphology Map:

   · Show up for work – show drive and the right attitude.

   · Be helpful, be accountable and lead by example.

   · Operate with humility and be endlessly curious.

   · Seek feedback and empower yourself to drive the changes that benefit you most.

   · Communicate with clarity and purpose.

   · Understand not only yourself but those you need to influence.

# BITE SIZE MORPHOLOGY

**CHAPTER 2:** Modifying your operating model

Tips for navigating this Morphology Map:

- Any change must be in service of your core purpose – it engenders belief and support.
- Minimize complexity and maximize efficiency.
- Implementation at a pace that matches the level of risk you are prepared to take.
- Communication and influencing is a constant – you must take your people with you.
- Seek feedback, listen and iterate your plan – it will drive the pace of adoption.
- Communicate and celebrate the progress you have made.

**CHAPTER 3:** Product or service diversification

Tips for navigating this Morphology Map:

- Understand your market, your buyers and what your competitors are up to.
- Have a process which enables you to make objective decisions and iterate.
- Be able to articulate the offering to your market: features, benefits, price and value.
- Engage existing and potential customers.
- Have a robust go-to-market plan, with sales and delivery teams in place and ready.
- Timing is everything, make sure your customers are ready and make sure you are too.

**CHAPTER 4:** Mergers and acquisitions

Tips for navigating this Morphology Map:

- Be clear on why – it must add value.
- Know what good looks like when selecting a target – if in doubt, don't do it.
- Make sure you balance the opportunity against the risk.
- Appoint the right advisers – and not just those who focus on the money.
- Consider all aspects of the deal when you get to your go/no-go decision points.
- Ensure you have a post deal integration plan that maximises value.
- Take everyone with you, in the right way, and at the right time.

**CHAPTER 5:** People

Tips for navigating this Morphology Map:

- Your purpose and people proposition must align – it builds trust and loyalty.
- People change needs to be at a pace that allows people to get on board.
- Your organizational design needs to support both your purpose and people proposition.
- If you don't have the right capabilities, go and find them.
- Look after your existing people – develop their capability where you can.
- Manage performance – if you can't change the people, change the people.
- Communicate thoughtfully and continuously – know your audiences.

**CHAPTER 6:** Culture

Tips for navigating this Morphology Map:

- Define the culture you need to deliver your purpose – engage your people in the process.
- Changing culture needs everyone to take part – devolve ownership.
- Make sure your operating model supports the culture you aspire to.
- Asking people to break old habits and create new ones takes time – be patient.
- Ensure there are consequences – both for role modelling and resisting.
- Changing culture is a long game – repeat, repeat, repeat until it becomes self-generating.

**CHAPTER 7:** Maximizing your personal impact

Tips for navigating this Morphology Map:

- Show up for work – show drive and the right attitude.
- Be helpful, be accountable and lead by example.
- Operate with humility and be endlessly curious.
- Seek feedback and empower yourself to drive the changes that benefit you most.
- Communicate with clarity and purpose.
- Understand not only yourself but those you need to influence.

# Chapter 8
# Bringing it all together

## Introduction

Standing still in today's business world is not an option. Every business needs to morph to survive and thrive. Every business will go through the five levers in this book multiple times over its lifetime. Those that don't won't stay around. Some levers will be pulled singularly, or it may well be a combination of different levers all being used at the same time. The point is that you should be actively thinking about which levers, and at what pace you need to be pulling them, to achieve your objectives.

Although each of the levers described in this book have a number of unique elements that need to be accommodated in your overall plan of action, there are also a number of themes that are common across all the levers.

## Understand the *why*

No lever can be successfully pulled without first understanding *why* it is you are choosing to take that action. It is vital that you have clarity on the problem you are looking to solve – whatever that might be. If you understand that, then you can be confident you will pull the right lever, or combination of levers, to get the outcome you want.

Having identified the *why*, it is imperative that you actively use it to communicate during all phases of your implementation plan. You can never over communicate. You need to ensure everyone knows why the changes are taking place and how they are in service of the outcomes identified.

# It takes leadership

Morphing is hard. It takes courage and resolve to embark on changing something. The status quo is always the easiest option but the key to impactful leadership is to do the right thing at the right time, even if the changes required are challenging.

As Jim Collins[9] pointed out, the very best leaders have a 'ferocious resolve, an almost stoic determination to do whatever needs to be done to make the company great'. But this stoic determination must embrace the humility required to change direction, or iterate plans based on the learning you get as you go. That humility and honesty needs to underpin your communication. Never forget to tell people how far you've come together, what you've learned along the way and what people can expect next – all framed by reminding them of why.

# Take your customers and people with you

The two most important elements of any business are your customers and your staff. Without them you have no business and no future. These are the core groups of people that you are communicating with and are leading. They aren't a homogenous group. Different segments will have different needs and concerns. Be mindful of that and plan your communication and engagement activities to differentiate between the generic messages that everyone needs to hear and the specific ones that need to be more targeted.

But always remember that your customers and staff have a voice as well – you need to listen and respond to their feedback as much, if not more, if you are to craft the messages you want them to hear.

# You have to have a plan

This entire book is predicated on the principle of the Morphology Maps helping you build a plan. A plan that identifies not only the things you can control, but also the things you need to try and influence in order to achieve your objectives. Each Map in this book is informed by

---

[9] J. Collins, *Good to Great*, First Edition, Random House Business, 4 October, 2001.

our experiences and battle scars. Your plan will not necessarily contain every component of a Morphology Map. But it will give you a solid start point for the development of your plan so that you can reach your outcomes faster. Without a plan, nothing happens.

The beauty of a plan is it not only articulates the *what, when* and *who*, but it also enables you to understand the interactions between concurrent activities. It ensures that the pace of change is recognized and underpins and brings to life the changes you are making. Share the plan so that everyone is clear on *what, when* and *who* – this shouldn't be a secret, it should be a blueprint for the outcomes you are working towards.

But don't fear the unexpected – the only certainty about the first draft of your plan is that it will be wrong, as it will be based on your best set of educated assumptions at that point in time. Amending and adapting the plan is not only OK, but actively encouraged. Make sure those educated assumptions become more refined and based on new insights, so that you are on even firmer footing as you plan your next set of actions.

# Define your destination, celebrate and learn

Why you are choosing to change is in service of the outcomes that you are hoping to achieve. These define your destination. It will have taken courage, resilience, determination, humility and lots of hard work to get there. You will have learned an enormous amount about yourself, the organization, its people, your customers and the market along the way. This is all priceless information for the next time you need to morph. Be proud that you reached your destination, and key milestones along the way. Celebrate this in your continued communication and engagement activities. And make sure that learning is fed into your next morph. Because there will be a next one. And another one after that. Because standing still is not an option.

# Epilogue

The drive to write this book came from a desire to share decades of experience; enabling you to benefit from our learning and deliver the outcomes you want faster. We want this book to be a practical tool to help support you and your business outcomes. We hope that you will refer back to the Morphology Maps as your guide to creating an impactful plan of action.

The start point for your plan will be specific to the situation you find yourself in and every set of outcomes will be unique to you. The lever or levers you chose to apply to effect the change you want to achieve will also be scenario specific. As discussed in Chapter 1, and brought to life in the image below, we are confident that there will be occasions where your plan will need a combination of elements drawn from across several of the Morphology Maps.

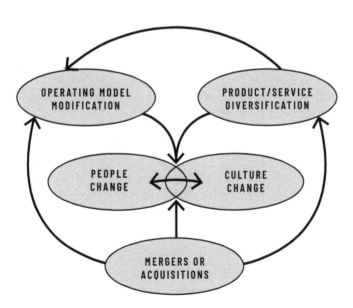

So, when you pick up your pen or hover your fingertips above your keyboard to start creating the plan that will morph your organization to the outcome you want to see, be aware that your start point may not be the only Morphology Map you need to consider. Refer to the others where you can see the potential for interdependency. The Maps signpost you to the building blocks you need as the foundation for your plan. And the best plans use these foundations to build in more detail so that everyone is clear on the specific activities, timelines, effort, interdependencies and outcomes the plan will deliver.

# Planning tips

Whilst planning is a fundamental skill for pretty much every role in organizations now, it still surprises us how the root cause for many of the turnarounds or failing change programmes that we work on has been because the fundamentals of good planning have been missed.

Now you may be an expert planner, in which case, close the book and get planning. But it seemed appropriate to share some of the common bear traps we've seen every type of organization fall into so that you can avoid them when it comes to pulling your plans together.

- Define your destination: your plan has only one aim – the destination you want to get to. We've seen too many plans get built from the start point – adding in building blocks and different steps in an attempt to include all the things that need to be covered in order to account for every eventuality. Planning starts with the end in mind and every activity included in your plan should be challenged in the context of how it will enable you to reach your destination faster, cheaper or to a higher standard.

- Requirements before solutions: at their simplest, change programmes exist to do three things – identify a problem, put in place a fix and make it stick so it endures on a sustainable basis. And the root cause of why most of them fail is because the problem wasn't identified properly in the first place (which means you have the wrong solution and it won't stick). You will notice that every Morphology Map has an activity designed to seek clarity or alignment on the control side. It is human nature to want to rush in and start doing stuff, so we appreciate it is counter intuitive to stop, check and reflect.

But time spent up front in a design phase is never wasted. By testing your assumptions and being clear about root causes up front, you can have confidence that when you move into delivery you can move at pace and are less likely to come unstuck. Create enough space in your plan to validate your assumptions at the outset.

- Taking people on the change journey isn't *just* about communications and engagement: this will be a major component, but it is just one of three critical activities. The first one is to conduct a change impact assessment. What is the scope of the change you are planning? Who are the impacted people? The second activity is to then consider what interventions are needed to mitigate those impacts and support the smooth and speedy adoption of the changes you are introducing. This will usually take the form of training or guidance. And the third activity is your communication and engagement plan. Together, these three are essential to successful delivery of the changes you are implementing and will span the entire duration of your plan – they will be the earliest thing you start, and the last thing you finish. If you don't bring your people and customers with you, you'll never reach your destination with the outcomes you were hoping for.

- Resourcing: delivering change isn't something that can be done in the margins of anyone's day job, if it is to be done well. You will need to allow time in your plan to find the resources you need – whether it is for designing solutions, overseeing delivery, managing the change or tracking progress and benefits. You might release internal resources which need backfilling or hire temporary resources. Whichever you choose, you will need time in your plan to get them up to speed and ready to drive the change forward. Equally, you need to be conscious of the fact that any change will demand attention, engagement, time and effort from those who are being affected by the changes taking place – and of course they all have day jobs too. This is critical to the pace at which you proceed – taking your people with you is a constant in every change lever.

- Sequencing and dependencies: timing matters. As each of the Maps show, there are some things you need to start before others, and some things you need to run in parallel. However, the Maps are just that, Maps that are a guide to help you think about when things need to be done. They are not prescriptive, particularly when considering the inter-relationship between the control side of the Map and the influence side of the Map. So use the Map as a guide but your plan needs to be clear about why and where things sit on your timeline, which then allows you to highlight dependencies between key activities and which ones are on the critical path to success. Being clear about the rationale for why these activities are linked is important, when you come to iterate your plan.

- Regular review and iteration: the only certain thing about your plan is that it will be wrong! Sorry, we know that's hard to hear. But it's the same principle as a budget, it is an educated guess at a fixed point in time. Your assumptions will get tested, which will necessitate iteration. The feedback loops through your change, communication and engagement activities will need to be responded to. Your plan is a living, dynamic thing. Our top tip here is never to plan at any level of detail for much more than three months in advance. Detail for the near future and blocks of activity further out. Otherwise, you will eat time and resources in constantly re-planning the whole thing every time you want to iterate. And don't forget to refer back to the Morphology Maps as you iterate. Is there an activity missing? Is there an inter-relationship that is not being addressed? Which stakeholders have you forgotten?

- Contingency: unless you are a genius, you'll have missed something in your plan. When you add to that the iteration that will inevitably come during implementation, and the fact that we are always hopelessly optimistic by nature, and you can be certain that it will take longer than you first think. But don't overload your plan with so much contingency that it dilutes pace, rather think about an overall timeline which has a baseline and stretch deadline. Plan for the baseline, aspire to the stretch.

# In summary

Morphing from one state to another is complex and challenging and the only way to get the outcomes you want is to commit to taking action and build a plan. A plan that is clear about what steps are required to deliver those outcomes. A plan that gets the right balance between things that you can control and what you need influence, and their respective timings. A plan that is reviewed regularly as you go about implementing it – recognizing that whilst your outcomes will stay fixed, the route you take to get to them will need to be dynamic. And you may find yourself at the start of what will be rolling waves of morphs for your organization.

Happy planning!

# Acknowledgments

As ever, this is the section in the book where we get to say thanks to those who helped bring the book to life.

First, to Alison Jones who saw the concept of Business Morphology and instantly loved it, and to the whole team at Practical Inspiration who have supported and guided us along the way.

To those people whose brains we picked in the early stages – Gary, Simon, Rob and Oli. You gave us the confidence that we were on to something, and some great case study content.

To the creative brains at Thisaway who took a brief from two people whose brains aren't just wired in that way and cracked the design of the Maps so they would work in a book format.

To Oryxalign, for being the most fabulous hosts for our regular meetings over the course of the past year as we developed the concept, the content and the plan (yes, we do listen to our own advice!).

To our beta readers Allan, Alun, Diana, Gary, Godfrey, Rob and Seth, who read the first draft and provided the invaluable feedback to make the version you have in your hands right now as good as it could be.

To Emeritus Professor Tim Morris for his generous foreword and the kind words from all those who provided us with endorsements.

To our partners for putting up with us sitting in a dark room writing, drawing and muttering to ourselves throughout the process.

And to each other – without which there would be no Business Morphology. We've laughed, wracked our brains, got stuck, got ourselves unstuck, and encouraged each other to get this done. And at no point was anyone harmed with a propelling pencil (an in-joke, humour us).

We hope you've enjoyed reading the book and that the Maps and the other insights help you navigate whatever challenges you face ahead in your own morphs, and you benefit from the battle scars of us having been in your shoes over the years.

Julie and Geoff

# Index

pace of implementation 24–26
people 17–18, 26–29, 75
progress 28–29
technology choices 23–24
outcomes 3, 5
    modifying your operating model
        18–19, 29
    people change 88

**P**

partnering, in product or service
    diversification 44
peer-to-peer interventions 99
people 7, 9, 73–74, 89, 118, 120, 123,
    125
    as advocates and salepersons 45, 48
    attraction and retention 79–80, 99,
        102, 103–105
    capability building 81–83
    communication and engagement
        17–18, 87
    and culture 92, 93, 97, 99–100,
        102–105
    efficiency 5
    leadership 74–75
    managing performance 83–86
    modifying your operating model
        17–18, 26–29, 75
    Morphology Map 58, 72
    motivation 107
    pace of change 78
    purpose and proposition
        alignment 75–78
    rational for people change 87–88
    role alignment 80–81
performance, management of 83–86
    and culture 94, 97
    and management of personal
        impact 112
personal impact, maximization of
    10, 107–108, 116, 118
    Morphology Map 106, 108, 110
    moving on 114–115

plan for 112–113
self-empowerment 110
showing up for work 108–109
taking ownership 109–110
understanding yourself and others
    110–112
pilot products/services 43, 46
plans 3, 6, 120–121, 123–124, 127
    for maximization of personal
        impact 112–113
    tips for 124–126
portfolios, of products and services
    33
post-acquisition integration 62–65
posters 94
pricing 43–44
private sector 9
problem identification 124
processes
    efficiency of 5
    mergers and acquisitions 54
    modifying your operating model
        19
    product or service diversification
        38–40
product lifecycle 33
    return on investment 40
product or service diversification 6,
    7, 33–34, 50, 103, 118, 123
    capability building 47–48
    funding and return on investment
        40–41
    innovation failure 49–50
    knowing your competition 35–37
    knowing your market and
        customers 34–35, 36–37
    market offering 42–44
    market planning 45–47
    Morphology Map 32
    people 75
    pre/post sales engagement and
        marketing 44–45
    process 38–40

## A quick word from Practical Inspiration Publishing...

We hope you found this book both practical and inspiring – that's what we aim for with every book we publish.

We publish titles on topics ranging from leadership, entrepreneurship, HR and marketing to self-development and wellbeing.

Find details of all our books at: www.practicalinspiration.com

 **Did you know...**

We can offer discounts on bulk sales of all our titles – ideal if you want to use them for training purposes, corporate giveaways or simply because you feel these ideas deserve to be shared with your network.

We can even produce bespoke versions of our books, for example with your organization's logo and/or a tailored foreword.

To discuss further, contact us on info@practicalinspiration.com.

 **Got an idea for a business book?**

We may be able to help. Find out more about publishing in partnership with us at: bit.ly/PIpublishing.

*Follow us on social media...*

 @PIPTalking

@pip_talking

@practicalinspiration

@piptalking

Practical Inspiration Publishing

Printed in the USA
CPSIA information can be obtained
at www.ICGtesting.com
JSHW051345201123
52413JS00008B/66

9 781788 605625